The Cotton Tree

Sahr Sankoh

The Cotton Tree
By Sahr Sankoh

Published by

Sankoh Publishing
PO Box 971
Reno, NV 89504

www. thecottontreesite.wordpress.com
© 2016 Sahr Sankoh
All rights reserved.

For permissions contact: isata8888@yahoo.com

Print and Ebook formatting by Jeny Ruelo of www.thefastfingers.com
Illustrations by donfreelanz of www.freelancer.com

ISBN: 978-0-9972469-1-9

CONTENTS

FOREWORD..v
HOW TO READ THIS BOOK...vii

The Entries

A Dose of Determination 1
A Very Rapey Christmas Carol 3
Airline Antics 5
As The World Turns, The Flu Returns 7
Bowl for Peace Before Your Pins Get Struck Down................................9
But Is It Just?...11
Care to Fly Malaysian Air?.. 13
Character Assassinated 15
Come Here My Love; Wait... Is That An Adam's Apple? 17
Compliment Battle Rap 20
Curse Of The Hollywood Pharaoh 22
Don't Clown With Ronald..24
Don't Shoot.. 26
Don't Tease Me, Tijuana! 28
Driving Culture in the USA 31
Evil Empire...33
Faith Tested, Love Approved 35
God Save the Wolf.. 38
Going Back to Thailand 43
Heartache in Hindustan..45
Hot Dog, Hot Dog, Hot Diggity Dog!!! 47
It's About To Go Down.. 49
Japanese Horror 52
Journalist's Code of Ethics 55
Love is Deaf, Dumb and Blind..57
Mass Hysteria. Just In Time For The Holidays 59

Moon River 61
Mr. Chi-City 64
Never Forget: 9-12 66
Panhandling Scammers 68
Pole Position 70
Public Bus Hassles.. 72
Rebating You in a Circle Jerk 74
Retirement Issues 76
Sino-Aussie relations on Rudd's Watch 78
Sleeping with the Enemy 80
Sneaker Wonderland.. 82
SNL Korea® 84
Something About a Glass of Orange Juice.................................... 86
Starbucks' Demeanor 88
Stem Cells! What Gives?..90
Still Off The Hook 92
Tails From The Auto Repair Shop 94
Tales from the Backside...96
Ten Hours Walking as a Woman in NYC 98
The Almighty Pat Robertson 100
The Block Is Hot... 102
The Cassette Tape Culture... 104
The Chicano Movement 106
 The Crime Wizards of Oz 108
The Food Babe.. 110
The Holiday Scammers 112
The Icarus Claus.. 114
The Wonderful World of Doritos® 117
These Colors Don't Run..119
Zone Out.. 121

SPOILERS 125

FOREWORD

To be honest, I'd rather read the works of some five or six new wave, avant-garde rhymers penning works I can digest, rather than biding my time at a sedentary pace to bring my own work into fruition. But it's better this way. I need a healthy outlet to exude my penmanship in a whimsical style.

With this book, I challenge you to dissolve your metrophobia. Metrophobia, if you haven't googled it yet, is an inherent fear of poetry. Hey, I don't blame you. This alliterate society competing with Twitter, Netflix, and Instagram, and even audio books, who needs to sit down and concentrate on a novel for enjoyment? Mentioning books in social circles is costly. But poetry?

If you can make it past a continual current of lines as you would when you read lyrics of your favorite songwriter, you'll realize that I leave little to the imagination until the last word. Allusive footprints tread throughout the book. You either identify with some event or you wind up looking it up. However, for whatever reason you're unable to follow the underlying messages in each poem, I've added a "spoiler" to draw you closer to the main idea. I don't have time to "analyze" any poetry, do you?

The charm to writing this book is the fun of juxtaposing or inserting current events in each poem. I balance nostalgia, coming of age, fantasy, controversial bits, opinions, and personal experiences hoping to maintain your viewership. All this without any of that sing song nursery rhyme cadence. If you're unhappy with this book, knowing several other writers that spin rhymes better, let me know. I'd love to join that fan club.

HOW TO READ THIS BOOK

For starters, let's discuss how not to take on this publication. No need to emerge into a trance of deep concentration. No need to absorb every line for the breadth of imagery and figurative language. Scarcely a reason to even pick apart metaphors and similes. You may ask yourself whether the point of view is the author's or an assumed character.

Throughout the entries, the period and the comma are here to guide you. Follow them. Basically, you're only reading sentences. Find the period or comma before reading each sentence and phrase, or else you may lose your train of thought. Sure, there's tone to consider; word choice to consider, etc. But this is light verse, not mesmerizing poetry. In my case, only essays in unmetered rhyme. Except for one poem, there are no fancy stanzas.

Depending on the poem, you may find yourself reading about different topics within the same poem. Yes, at times, there is a sharp turn of topics without as much as transitional word to lead you so be prepared. Otherwise, check for the main ideas in the piece unless it's a storyline.

If that weren't enough, look at the complementing illustrations to get a grasp of the poem's theme.

The last section of the book are the spoilers in which I've enclosed a synopsis of each poem.

There you go. Should be smooth sailing. Find Dot and Comma for each sentence. Search for the main idea, look for the sharp twists of subject matter. And don't invest so much time in imagery. This is light verse, not poetry.

Excerpt from Sleeping with the Enemy

Scripture dictates that humans must love their sister and brother,
   [break in thought marked with a comma]
but I haven't found a verse implying we should trust each other.
   [complete thought marked with a period]
If it weren't the religious texts depicting the plight of Elijah,
I'd assume most tragedies resembled Samson and Delilah.
Due to naked vulnerabilities, | who wants to uncover
the calculated deception of a jilted lover? |
   [basic theme of the poem]
I have compassion for the star-studded figures in the public eye.
Celebrities hemorrhage as their reputations die.
| I cringed when the gossip hounds at TMZ were unfurling
the controversies regarding Mel Gibson and Donald Sterling. |
   [celebrities used for supporting examples]

Excerpt from Curse of the Hollywood Pharaoh

the glorious shrine and relics of Egypt's world renowned
king ever to send contemporary exhumers hell-bound.
The mummy rumor's sound naïve — even to the superstitious,
but the subsequent deaths of the discovers left me suspicious.
Since Hollywood cashes checks from fact-distorting,
why not reconsider the curse of Billy Bob Thornton?
[topic shift: King Tut to Billy Bob Thornton's Curse]
Strange how many of his co-stars died to a premature measure:
Bernie Mac, John Ritter, J.T. Walsh, Heath Ledger.
Although two male actors dodged Billy's deadly mojo,
don't discount the therapy they both had to undergo.
Morgan Freeman from a car crash, Patrick Swayze from cancer,
so what's a second opinion from the local necromancer?
Thornton's female co-stars haven't suddenly left the earth.
In fact, Halle Berry's undergone a nerve-wracking child birth,
[topic shift: Billy Bob Thornton's Curse to Halle Berry's child birth]

The Entries

A DOSE OF DETERMINATION

Adamant to purchase a thirty two ounce of a limited **Listerine**®'s
Forest Mint mouthwash and flip flops at **Walgreens**®,
I revved up the **Sentra**®, tuner set to **Sirius**® radio,
but the road blocks left me unsure of which way to go.
Funny how seldom toll roads are under construction,
and highway legislation goes unchallenged at each state function.
After a ten minute query for directions at a **Sunoco**® station,
I proceeded to race off to my intended destination.
 As I coasted in circles for an ample parking spot,

I grabbed a greased skid space near a bag some shopper forgot.
Hoisted out of the car, then my eyes took in a sketch
of a hawk diving into a pigeon for its midday catch.
The pigeon sunk, dazed, the hawk swooped down for the kill,
seized the prey's chest with its talons, pecking the head with its bill.
Honking the horn scared the predator away, for the moment,
enabling the stunned pigeon some sense of atonement.
That check-out line was longer than a Easter Sunday fellowship.
So I peeled open a tabloid to read the latest gossip,
despite the "has been" celebrity stories I had wanted to peruse,
page forty produced a woman riddled with a thousand tattoos
desperate to conceal porphyria[1] , or sunlight-induced
skin blistering, as a walking canvas for an ego boost.
Eighty thousand dollars in artwork to overcome depression
was nothing to this surfer who rode the wave to progression:
a fifteen foot tiger shark tore off the arm of a young teenager
but she refused to let the hapless tragedy upstage her.
Counting two arm surgeries and a six night hospital stay,
within a month she fled to the call of the ocean melee.
Fast forward five years, she displayed a tremendous transition
Winning second place in a worldwide surfing competition.
I was half hoping that pigeon found its own victory
yet I found it unmoving, headless, and no longer in agony.
And I cited seven decapitated birds in its wake.
The strong stay determined to the missions they take.

---

1   Porphyria, a rare hereditary disease in which the blood pigment hemoglobin is abnormally
metabolized.

A VERY RAPEY CHRISTMAS CAROL

As Thanksgiving day fades, we embrace our peers,
unlike our self-serving Black Friday antics terrifying cashiers.
Rather, thoughts of frothy egg nog and comfy get-togethers
where we exchange gifts and warm blessings for future endeavors.
We share an evening of plastic smiles that make your heart harden.
Do you recall the days spent learning songs in kindergarten?
And we had to assume roles for Dickens's *Christmas Carol*?
Remember the poinsettias and, the itchy green and red apparel?
And then, there's the Christmas carol outlawed in public schools.
The carol that subjugates, ridicules, and breaks dating rules.
"Baby, It's Cold Outside" was penned at a housewarming gathering;
a time when a Mikey Finn cocktail trumped a Singapore Sling.

1944. An era of Sinatra, Hitler, and the onset of baby boomers
born into the new world by unsuspecting drug consumers.
"Say, what's in this drink?" the lady voiced out her suspicion.
Her suitor deflected the question to misdirect her intuition.
"No cabs to be had out there." His insisting no rides were available
can be interpreted that the "wolf" was feeling unassailable.
As the "mouse" blatantly rejected him, he asked if he could "move in closer".
Despite the woman's unrelenting chants, nothing stirred his composure.
To be fair, the terms "mouse" and "wolf" are employed for the basis
the roles can be reversed. (And that offsets the op-ed pages).
The counter-argument contends that the mouse wanted to stay,
and, in the eyes of the predator, rendered herself as unbridled prey.
But the wolf's cajoling antics can be depicted as irritating.
In the mouse's defense---that argument is also worth debating.
The rights were sold to Columbia Pictures. Were they in the wrong?
Especially after taking home an Oscar for best original song?
Can the light hearted approach to date rape appear any duller
if it's directed by Hitchcock[2] and shot in Technicolor?
Should we condone song lyrics as hazy as the London fog?
Should we take a closer inspection of our host's egg nog?
Have the times made the song appear far too conservative
in the wake of new wave artists who pledge to stay alternative?
I hope the song is promoted for upcoming year end concerts.
Not as a provocative anthem aimed towards chasing skirts.
Its ambiguous song matter doesn't mean it averts
its moral responsibility in the world of dating standards.

---

2   Alfred Hitchcock, an English film director and producer.

AIRLINE ANTICS

We frequent flyers may have constantly mulled over the question
of whether passengers should be coddled into using discretion.
Unruly traveler anecdotes flood the newspapers often,
but one temper tantrum onboard drove the nail in the coffin.
Chairman Cho Yang Ho, while in the comforts of a cabin deluxe,
quizzed a flight attendant on how to serve macadamia nuts.
Upon failing the question, the **Korean Air**® executive demanded
the captain deplane the crewmember, leaving him stranded.
Abusing privileges warranted Cho a series of felonies
given she "provoked a flight delay" said aviation authorities.
In other news **US Airways**®[3] dealt with a deranged passenger
who lugged about a forty pound pig to accompany her.

---

3   US Airways, now defunct.

Her pot bellied companion relieved itself in the aisle.
The captain decided putting "wings on pigs" just wasn't his style.
Eventually she ushered herself from the craft without apology.
She even acted in confines of an updated DOTs[4] policy.
Prohibiting "emotion support animals" won't cause an impact.
Carriers are allowed to interpret the Animal Welfare Act.
The advent of disruptive flight entries started to rise
to embarrass prima donnas flying the friendly skies.
USA Today compiled a list of the typical airline trolls
with self-indulgent actions that tax on unsuspecting souls.
The juvenile "Rear Seat Kicker," "The Mad Bladder,"
that blue movie viewer who pretends porn doesn't matter,
"Overhead Bin Snatcher," "180 Degree Seat Recliner,"
"Inattentive Guardian, "Carry-On Bag Offender,"
"Pungent Foodie", "Boozer", "Inappropriate Undresser",
"Armrest Hogger", "Queue Jumper", "Touchy Feely Molester."
It's less likely that the top physicians of the City of Hope
can offer homeopathy to redouble a flier's means to cope.
Over the counter **Tiger Balm**® or **Vicks**® menthol kills
repulsive odors after applying its contents under the nostrils.
Assuage the kick boxer with breath mints on the cheap.
Dupe the chatterbox by feigning to fall asleep.
Tell the "Recliner" you overheard his seat's falling apart.
Trip the "Queue Jumper" before he gets a running start.
In flight movies work wonders when bribing parents.
Stifle unbridled laughter hoping the "Undresser" takes offense.
Offer to buy a drink to get dibs on the coveted armrest.
Start wheezing and coughing before you get caressed.
Sadly, "Hints from Heloise[5]" fail to cover all occasions,
so here's to you—all the best—to monitor your patience.

---

4   DOT, Department of Transportation.
5   A once syndicated newspaper column "Hints from Heloise".

AS THE WORLD TURNS, THE FLU RETURNS

Mexico experienced a tranquility unfelt in decades,
struck with temporary amnesia to her daily escapades.
Her capital, a bustling megalopolis world renowned
as the most densely populated, barely uttered a sound.
Cacophonies of cab horns reduced to an echoing whisper;
local meteorologists insisted the city air was crisper.
As opposed to forecasting the brewing miasma
of motorized carcinogens prone to induce asthma.
Petty crime nosedived to shuddering lows
while nationwide panic following influenza grows.

Robbing Pedro hoping to pay Pablo
or thwarting the curse of the greenhouse Diablo,
became low priority when Mexico's president,
Felipe Calderon, announced that every resident
remain homebound for a period of five days,
while clinics kept vigil to verify every malaise.
The worldwide reaction to the swine flu pandemic
conveyed how rash judgments create problems quick:
Egypt's injunction resulted in impoverished herders
waving pitch forks at police, protesting livestock murders.
The Metropark Hotel administered a heinous weeklong
quarantine of its guests in Wanchai, Hong Kong.
Critics felt the hotel's prudent actions came too soon
while local officials were mindful of that familiar tune.
An avian flu outbreak showered a poultry farm,
prompting experts to issue a low vaccine alarm.
However no foreign nations demanded a stern extradition
like China, while enraged Mexicans were drawn to petition
and refused to take part in the Shanghai trade fair
due to shunning their citizens with unacceptable care.
China defended its stance by refusing to tolerate any strain
of influenza virus and continue its quarantine campaign.
While both nations act like jilted lovers in diplomatic relations,
scientists pledge to seek a cure for the hospitalized patients.

BOWL FOR PEACE BEFORE YOUR PINS GET STRUCK DOWN

Finish your text message on your **Motorola**®
while I'll fetch another bottle of champagne cola[6].
Now one moment your whole body was numb by nightfall,
the next you were beckoned by a haunting call.
Like a scream? Phone call? Then what? Specify.
Visions of manic depressives and a ubiquitous eye?
You fell into a trance, escaped your physical frame,
spoke in radio waves—what, You're incoherent…explain!
Stop panicking! I know you want to be serious.
But even that pysch major's convinced you're delirious,

---

6   Champagne cola is a sweet carbonated beverages produced mainly in the tropics

telling the whole campus about channeling spirits from within.
Can you channel your inner zombie to hit a bowling pin?
Your Frankenstiff arm swing is the worst on earth
with a routine so obscene, I can't determine your worth.
Now we're the humiliation of the bowling leagues
with your floppy clown shoes and gypsy fatigues.
Either channel Houdini, doctor up some hat tricks,
or do yourself a favor and cut the theatrics!
Calm down a second. Here's a spearmint **Certs**®
before you dare reckon you're competing with experts.
Not even by the grace of a cardinal's prayers.
We bowl to clear our minds of morbid current affairs.
In the vein of Virginia Tech[7], serial killers resurface:
four gunmen in central Arkansas without a purpose
left two dead with firearms found on college property.
Detroit wonders if their mayor was convicted properly.
Kilpatrick[8], lying under oath, pleaded guilty
to obstruction of justice, and got his paws filthy
attempting to strong arm a hired detective,
now sentenced to four months plus a cost effective
million dollar fine for an outrageous sex scandal.
These day to day calamities grow harder to handle.
I've got the check—hey, you think that perhaps
next time we do Caribbean, we try the veggie wraps?
Check out these sides—seasoned green beans,
the infamous black beans with rice, baked plantains.
Make sure those benevolent spirits can surely guide us
to the best entrées Texas Carib can provide us.
Just make sure your newfound clairvoyance
doesn't continue to be an annoyance.

---

7   Virginia Tech shootings occurred on April 16, 2007,
8   Kwame Kilpatrick, a former Michigan state representative and Democratic mayor of Detroit

BUT IS IT JUST?

On December 16, one peculiar article appeared
in this particular week's account of the "News of the Weird."
One of four suspects was held in protective custody
for hand gun possession charges in Mercer County.[9]
Authorities stated a gun and a bottle of prescription codeine
were confiscated by law enforcement at the crime scene.
Defense attorney Caroline Turner moved to abort
bail charges on the handicapped suspect in court.
Marcus Hubbard, diagnosed by a state physician,

---

9   Mercer County, a **county** located in the U.S. state of New Jersey.

had long since suffered from a severe spinal condition
that denies him use of either of his hands;
however, his $35,000 bail until his court date still stands.
Prosecution holds the New Jersey man can still face gun crimes
despite his disability, as reported in the *Trenton Times*.
Upon being pulled over for a red light violation,
police spotted the revolver when checking his driver's registration.
Defense attorneys insisted that the judgment on Hubbard stems
from the man's pleading ignorance of the stolen items.
The judge relented only in lowering the invalid's bail
despite having spent four months of taxpayers' money while in jail.
Commenters are baffled as to why the judge would uphold the bounty
until the reader learns that Mercer is a cash-strapped county.
Scrolling through an article posted by the *Sharon Herald* shows
government subsidies for libraries embrace record lows.
Contractors file suit to recover money the county owes,
and other accounts spiraling Mercer into financial woes.
Putting fundraising methods in the equation, must this
conclusion draw us into thinking it's an act of injustice?
Turner holds that prosecution exaggerates a clause
used to enforce constructive possession laws,
exacting charges on individuals that indirectly possess
contraband despite being in a criminal court of duress.
The argument that the system is, in fact, chaotic
in its handling of the case also defies logic:
although it's impossible for Hubbard to brandish a handgun,
he still stands as an abetting accomplice in the long run.
Withholding a testimony leading to a conviction
is grounds to harbor Hubbard, even with his affliction.
Since all four suspects involved are in denial,
as a team they should all await their trial.

CARE TO FLY MALAYSIAN AIR?

The ominous cloud shadowing Malaysian Air
set the carrier in travesties beyond repair.
Although the company is not alone in losing clientele,
In 2014, they endured a ride on a nightmarish carousel.
Flight 370 somehow vanished without a trace
after losing contact with the company's interface.
Airport traffic controllers fought in vain paging
the Boeing 777 scheduled to land in Beijing.
The unspeakable occurred as awaiting families feared:
Authorities failed to determine where the aircraft disappeared.
Shares plunged, finding itself caught in a downward spiral
as mounting conspiracy theories went viral.

Terrorists subdued the captain, and rerouted the flight
was the most feasible likelihood that surfaced to the light.
No extremist militias have taken credit for the mishap.
Suspicions hold the craft was shrouded in an airborne "body wrap".
An invisibility cloak designed by evil innovative scientists
pledged to whack AIDS researchers on their hit lists.
Others contend North Korea concealed the plane's location,
planning to demand ransom amid the world's frustration.
Investigators involved in the uncanny mission even dare
to suggest the craft may have disintegrated in mid-air.
Some theorists conclude that a supernatural force
navigated the Beijing bound jetliner off course.
For this Malaysia hired shamans to investigate
whether the undetected passengers met their fate.
With coconuts in mid-air, the witch doctor pleaded,
chanted, and prayed for spiritual guidance needed.
"Bamboo binoculars", flying carpets and a magic boat
made hecklers surmise Aladdin did the dead man's float.
The government was ridiculed all over the Internet
for the most bizarre spectacle performed at the airport yet.
Despite this courtroom of controversy with fate as its judge
If the prosecution persists, why should the jury budge?

CHARACTER ASSASSINATED

John H. Richardson writes, "This is life among the alpha males where the tournament of egos", as noted, always prevails. The Esquire™ magazine that showcased none other than the leggy Cameron Diaz splashed onto its August cover, detailed the "afterlife" of the mighty Lance Armstrong who denied to the world that he committed no wrong. But his detractors claim to the sports world he doesn't belong. Public opinion dismissed him as singing the same old song. How can this man carry seven consecutive cycling titles without any enhancement drugs as our favorite idols? Shallow faith forbids contemplation over the possible chance that a dying victim brooding in the hospital

with a malignant tumor in his testes fighting for his life
become a beacon worldwide for patients under the knife.
Once touted by onlookers as an unrelenting champion.
Tour de France's Icarus determined to conquer the Sun.
The man lauded as cancer's most valiant trailblazer
pressured to resign from his own fundraiser.
Steve Jobs syndrome. To coin a needed phrase
conveying the shallow outlook hypocrisy displays.
The world loathes an indefatigable winner
to the extent that mistrust warrants him a sinner.
Since the tour's outbreak, most relied on amphetamines,
or ample steroids to transform themselves into road-racing machines.
Jealous peddlers viewed Armstrong chastise them to the top
with crass determination throbbing in his veins nonstop.
Accusers balked that he used performance inducers,
namely life-threatening EPOs[10] for blood-oxygen boosters.
How is it that the Worldwide Sports Federation
has the right to deny athletes on mere speculation?
Was it the sheer envy of his former two-wheeling cronies
encouraged by supporters to give suspect testimonies?
Lawsuit after lawsuit helped sustain his feigned innocence
until conscience bit his psyche, and his knee-jerk pretense.
Guilt pinned him to confession, spinning heads on Oprah.
Misled sponsors Radio Shack®, Nike®, Nissan®, Coca-Cola ®
escorted him in shame, spurred on by the salivating media
to an obscure destination uncharted by Expedia.
But undeterred cancer patients recognized their catalyst of hope
in genuine videos, surrendering his pride to cope.
To walk away from millions and acclaim for a delicate crisis
that mirrors your integrity is nothing short of priceless.

---

10   Erythropoietin, glycoprotein produced by the kidneys also known as EPO.

COME HERE MY LOVE; WAIT...
IS THAT AN ADAM'S APPLE?

Pinching myself fiercely, no longer dreaming,
I was utterly possessed by Nell Carter's[11] demon.
Leaped into the **Sentra**®, hungry man on board,
scouting for eateries eight bucks can afford.
After idling in traffic, I decided to park it
by the **China Chef**® or the **Boston Market**®.
An empathic "no" to MSG, I'm so in denial,

---

11   Nell Carter, an American singer and actress.

Boston's a la carte menu can be worth the while
Ignoring my intuition, I proceeded to BM
where I'm less likely to find cat hair in my phlegm.
Six minutes away from being famine-stricken,
I'm served creamed spinach, a quarter pound chicken.
I'm strong to the finish 'cause I eat my creamed spinach,
but will this creamed spinach portion diminish?
No point telling an adult to gobble up his veggies,
yet this slime is bottomless, and it's making me edgy.
And this rotisserie chicken is as limp and flaccid
as a noodle--heaven help me find a cherry antacid!
No luck. No question, I'm a fast food junkie
It's making my wordplay and my intestines funky.
Go ahead, introduce me to all things gastronomic
until my frisky appetite turns platonic.
But could you fetch me a box of cinnamon **Altoids®**?
CVS® has them right below the two dollar tabloids.
There's a ten to one chance you'll find my fingerprints
on a tin box of those "curiously strong mints."
Last night I headed to the Absinthe Café downtown
in search of corruption in an evening gown.
Plenty of eye candy, The Host? An excellent songbird,
but I had to restrain from champagne and using the L-word.

Most guys at the venue thought it was downright shady
to compete with a lady to find a lady,
but I continued chatting until conversations went stale,
half wishing I ordered a Molotov cocktail,
convinced that lesbians spoke their own lingo:
just another obstacle unearthed being single.
Afterwards I exchanged words with a Cajun lady
who, for rhyme's sake, was aptly named Katie.

Judging by her finesse, she was surely a winner;
then she invited me to meet her spouse for dinner.
The cougar insisted that we exchange recipes;
her husband was a fan of foreign delicacies.
Regrettably, I'm aware that I can be naïve
but, based on the situation, I was left to believe
that Katie was a lady who enjoyed thrill seeking
with her voyeur husband, albeit every weekend.
Maybe I misunderstood last night's discussion.
Maybe my cocktail was spiked with Robitussin®.
Maybe I was born the day after yesterday.
But I doubt I'll return to the Absinthe Café.

COMPLIMENT BATTLE RAP

If you're an Eminem fan, you might have seen the movie "8 Mile".
The film glorified battle rap and the art of lyrical freestyle.
Freestyle is impromptu poetry set to a syncopated beat
or acapella, whereas battle rap pummels the rival into defeat.
Now, verbal acoustics shun beats, making the vibe theatrical.
Recitals over improvisation; vivid tall tales are allegedly factual.
However, a new subgenre of mainstream battle rap emerged
in a few varsity leagues in several countries suddenly surged.
Slaying your opponent in a hailstorm of compliments,

exchanging pleasantries with a taste for vengeance,

watching these charm school warriors deeply affected

the hip hop audience into engaging in the unexpected.

Take the promotional face-off between Rone and Pat Stay[12]

sharing strawberry smoothies on a midsummer's day.

Probably the most hilarious battle I ever witnessed

was when both opponents deserved an encore at the Hopscotch Fest.

Observe how Rone the challenger seamlessly hustles

with rhyme and wit to praise the champion's muscles.

"Is it the proteins you digest? The low weight—the high reps?

Did you give away your bed? Do you sleep on an incline press?"

Pat Stay steps up the ante exuding years of practice

so that the crowd stays enthralled by his lyrical theatrics.

"His daddy and mommy are rich.

If I had a body like his, I'd be the underwear model for Abercrombie and Fitch."

The Greely and Barry Bonza bout sounded like a twisted

confession of true bromance as the battle persisted.

Not insinuating that those sentiments even existed,

but I tuned out the players when the vibe got limp-wristed.

Greely stings him with "Whoever said Barry's a regular person

forgot to mention he's an excellent version."

And Barry's response, "Being better than me at bars is something you have to deal with,

and no matter how hard I try, it's never going to equal up to this Greel shit."

The compliment version of battle rap is still a work in progress.

but I'm glad it's off and running like the Pony Express.

---

12   Rone and Pat Stay, **King of the Dot** Entertainment, also known as **KOTD**, is a rap battle league founded
      in Toronto, Canada in 2008.

CURSE OF THE
HOLLYWOOD PHARAOH

Four months left for the King Tutankamen exhibit
here in Dallas Metroplex, and I have some time to visit
the glorious shrine and relics of Egypt's world renowned
king ever to send contemporary exhumers hell bound.
The mummy rumors sound naïve—even to the superstitious,
but the subsequent deaths of the discoverers left me suspicious.
Since Hollywood cashes checks from fact-distorting,
why not reconsider the curse of Billy Bob Thornton?
Strange how many of his co-stars died to a premature measure:
Bernie Mac, John Ritter, J.T. Walsh, Heath Ledger.
Although two male actors dodged Billy's deadly mojo,

don't discount the therapy they both had to undergo:
Morgan Freeman from a car crash, Patrick Swayze[13] from cancer,
so what's a second opinion from the local necromancer?
Thornton's female co-stars haven't suddenly left the earth
In fact, Halle Berry's undergone a nerve-wracking child birth,
exasperated that her diabetes would complicate the matter,
but Berry exhaled in joy watching that glass ceiling shatter
in the form of a healthy, bouncy baby daughter,
so neither the mother nor the child became a martyr.
Besides, she can receive prenatal care of any proportion,
unlike the fetal victims of an pauper's abortion.
Not to be misconstrued with old fashioned tactics
involving a copper coat hanger and a pissy yellow mattress.
This caper involves three birth control pills every three days,
anticipating bleeding to complete the phase.
Although a new investigation the government fails to implement,
these situations exist, unwarranted, without consent,
without much hope solving a riddle or finding an explanation
to the societal ills that plague our generation.

---

13   At the time of writing, the aforementioned actor was alive. RIP

DON'T CLOWN WITH RONALD

I've been a childhood fan of my local **McDonalds**®
back when Jackson had an afro the size of Ronald's.
No different than your average three year old child,
whenever seeing the "Golden Arches" we turn wild,
Unaware of how the fast food chain destroys us
apart from the McDonald land song that annoys us:
"You deserve a break today", so goes the tune,
Parents pause to themselves knowing it will die soon.
Despite the ongoing lawsuits McDonalds remains defiant
as the world's number one fast food giant.
Of course, the press hardly mentions the charities

the restaurant provides, it's among the rarities
of establishments known to enable the youth.
This goes unknown although they've published the truth:
Reaching the world's impoverished children worldwide
with a hospital on wheels they sought to provide.
This mobile offers a laboratory, a reception hall,
two examination rooms, if needed at all.
Aside from giving pamphlets of health education,
either medical or dental to uplift a third world nation.
 I'm aware of *Super Size Me* and its two hour parable:
A regimen based on Mickey D's is strictly unbearable.
But who's forcing us to buy their McDonaldland shake?
Their Quarter Pounder? Some chance we take!
I'd rather rant about a no-name franchise and their buffalo wings
but I'm aware of the terror that cholesterol brings.
Ever seen a slim trim McDonald's employee
who benefited from the store being all he could be?
Not! Too many roly-poly wannabee Angelina Jolie's
living the fat life of SNL's Matt Foleys.
I don't care if Ronald gives you his lipstick frown,
do your best to cast the Double Cheeseburger down
There's no point in seeing obesity take lives
while an unstoppable network thrives!

DON'T SHOOT

Rumor had it that the antics of a runaway slave
instigated the infamous massacre that drove him to the grave.
Scathing insults as well as blunts objects were thrown
at the British soldiers on watch made it hard to condone
unrelenting protests while the evening progressed,
Crispus Attucks[14] was shot dead with a bullet to the chest.
As we spun the grandfather clock to August 9, 2014,
caution tape unwound throughout the police scene,
reporters badgered onlookers wondering who staged the assault
that left Mike Brown motionless and bleeding on the asphalt.

---

14   Crispus Attucks, an African-American man killed during the Boston Massacre, making him the first
      casualty of the American Revolution.

Officer Darren Wilson was allegedly involved in a tussle

and absolved by entry wounds to the skull, neck and forearm muscle.

But that account of the case may prove incorrect.

Brown's autopsy insisted he was fleeing suspect.

Namely that his garments showed no clue of gunshot residue,

once we weigh the pathologist's point of view.

At the time of this writing, the verdict is in a state of unknown,

Besides, the unrest has shifted to a volatile tone:

Flash grenades. Tear gas. Blood resistant riot gear.

All pledge to quell the biggest riot of the year.

On site reporters gave this worldwide attention.

while Wilson remained incognito on paid suspension.

Palestinians advised rioters on managing tear gas attacks.

Beijing criticized Washington's mistreatment of blacks.

Even the Umbrella Revolution[15] did their best to follow suit

with posters that gestured that cried, "Hands Up, Don't Shoot!".

Not only was an apology offered by the Chief of Police,

Chief Jackson tried locking arms with activists chanting, "No justice, no peace".

It's baffling how Ferguson's finest brought their beloved canine pets

while donning "I am Darren Wilson" charm bracelets.

Facebook® posters added their own flavor of dissent,

wondering which photograph would the media present.

Each portraits offered to upset a preconceived premise

that the individual was born to play the societal menace.

Opportunists among activists displayed typical theatrics.

Tibetan monks and senators jailed for Civil Rights tactics.

Even his mother caught the in-laws profiting from the misery;

Grandma sold t-shirts and trinkets, claiming she was a licensee.

Despite the state-enacted curfews, violated constitutional rights,

the judge presiding over the case could take the unrest to new heights.

---

15   Umbrella Revolution, protests in Hong Kong against proposed electoral reform which was perceived to limit the democratic participation of the people of Hong Kong.

DON'T TEASE ME, TIJUANA!

There I was, sifting my fork in fettuccine Alfredo,
wondering what was left to encounter in San Diego:
there had to be some childish mischief to get into.
The Gas Lamp District? Too polished. I've already been to
the Trophy Lounge nested by the **Holiday Inn**®
where IT hubbies whine and navy wives sin.
So, facing the last leg of the weekend at the Heartbreak Hotel,
I'd head further south for some unadulterated hell.
Where else on a Sunday can you encounter a reckless nirvana
without considering San Dog's[16] sister, Viva Tijuana?

---

16   San Dog, local slang for San Diego.

I jumped on the trolley, dressed in a modest profile.
Reached the last stop: TJ! An unmanned turnstile?
Shocked for a minute. Realized it made sense:
I chose boyish adventure at a man's expense.
Changed dollars to pesos. Spotted a steak quesadilla
but the Lonely Planet warned me of contracting diarrhea.
So I motioned good bye to my taco vendor friends;
don't need a full blown case of Montezuma's revenge[17].
I made it to Revolution Avenue. (picture the Big Easy[18]).
Bourbon Street. Same theme. Twice as sleazy.
Underage boozers. Mariachi clubbers.
Unlicensed nip & tuckers. Transgendered money grubbers.
Quilt-laden elves pledging for handouts.
Aggressive cop shake downs for unruly bouts.
I sauntered into one of the main drag's iguana cantinas.
They were offering ninety-nine centavo[19] Cadillac Margaritas!
Floor tiles peppered with watery, cigarette ashes.
Televised dog races stirred men with pomaded moustaches.
While sponging off the salt with my third lime wedge
this alluring missy sent my hormones on edge,
jutting her goodies in a silky negligee,
as inviting as a spicy getaway in Monterrey.

I'd be a foal without a strand of horse sense
not to approach her, charged with liquid confidence.
Into a crowded dance floor I fell in sync to the drums
of meringue rhythms as beckoning nightfall succumbs.
She giggled at my two step but followed my stride.
My periphery noticed her signaling a woman sitting aside.

---

17   Montezuma's Revenge, a jocular term for travelers' diarrhea.
18   The Big Easy, a nickname for the American city of New Orleans, Louisiana.
19   Centavo, a cent in Spanish.

That girl embraced my ribs as my target pulled me closer,
Not suspecting the reaction that suddenly froze her.
Her accomplice slipped her fingers into my pocket.
I let her. Then followed her stealthy hand to block it.
I squeezed her wrist, sprang out of the dance circle,
heard them scream, "Idioto!" Their faces turning purple.
After paying my tab I left the smoky premises
realizing any local can be an opportune nemesis.
Hotheaded as I was, I sauntered into **Sanborns**[®20] to forget
my escapade and seek refuge in a Spanish omelet.
I nursed a Corona and watched this nine year old
playing with oblong blocks before an idea rolled.
We both played three games of makeshift **Genja**[®]
before he finally asked the focus of my agenda.
"Gringo, why you here? You like marijuana?"
He produced a nickel bag from his tattered parka.
Then an observing cop motioned the boy to discontinue,
from outside the glass panel, his drug peddling venue.
The boy grimaced, "You go home? You go frontera?"
At once a joker intervened that wore blush and mascara.
Judging by the ring of cumstains on his collar,
Tia Hotpants worked hard for the almighty dollar.
His throaty voice, demanding, "You go to the border!"
followed by curious eyes sensing brewing disorder.
I jetted with intent to return to the Heartbreak,
besides my **Rockport**[®] trodden feet started to ache.
Onward to customs, no one cared for protesting
the camped families that stayed near the entrance nesting.
Homeland Security checked my ID. Then I flagged a cab driver,
thankful for simply being a day-to-day survivor.

---

20   Sanborns, a large **restaurant**, retail, pharmacy and department store chain located in Mexico

DRIVING CULTURE IN THE USA

Elisabeth Rosenthal, in an article, offered a looming variety
of trends implying the American shift to a carless society.
Despite basing her findings from Doug Short of Advisor Perspectives,
I doubt our government will approach any transportation objectives.
Japan celebrated the fiftieth anniversary of their famous bullet train
while taxpayers struggled to prolong the Northeast Maglev campaign[21].
Assuming domestic airline corporations on the sidelines teems
with lobbyists poised to thwart train legislation by all means,
the working middle class remains smug in a luxury sedan,
heckling staffers off to work in a sponsored charter van.

---

21 Northeast maglev, A 39 Mile (64 km) project has been proposed linking Camden Yards in Baltimore and
    Baltimore-Washington International (BWI) Airport to Union Station in Washington, D.C

Gas prices plummeting in a downward spiral doesn't help.
The street side catcalling video going viral doesn't help.
The import scene is thriving. The Fast and the Furious franchise
showed kids Vin Diesel was a racer god on the rise.
If anything, give public transportation its undue credit.
Ask any long-standing commuters whether he or she regrets it.
Would you rather be a teenager mother gripping a bus pass
and toting a child or an impatient cabbie waiting to pump gas?
As for me, I'd rather reach my intended destination
in whatever means that offers the least frustration.
The Google Corporation has been experimenting lately
on driver less vehicles that pride themselves on road safety.
Although driverless technology is legal in three states,
corrections must be met to secure nationwide mandates.
Nowadays, mobile ridesharing applications caused a rift
in the taxi-aggressive world with firms Uber and Lyft.
Their patrons no longer endure time management sacrifices
along with snotty attitudes that complement inflated prices.
Green technology took flight in the dawn of the '08 recession.
Experts and fiscal charts point out Tesla's uphill progression.
A new car has surfaced that is so environmentally friendly,
Rumor has it founder Elon Musk bit his lip in envy.
Ellie Zolfagharifard for Mail Online states that our
muscle sports car contender runs on saltwater horsepower.
"No hydrogen cells involved" means no potential explosion,
albeit the storage cells remain prone to brackish corrosion.
Armchair speculators refute the premise that the New World vulture
whets its talons to dismantle automobile culture.
Car ownership will resurge to unprecedented heights
once the driver spark in Generation Millennium ignites.

EVIL EMPIRE

The world locked arms together advocating Occupy Wall Street.
but somehow the mismanaged movement crumbled beneath their feet.
Amid freedom fighters and protesters, business moguls laugh
knowing local activists remain too ill-informed to stomach the wrath.
The lovechildren of Upton Sinclair[22], the devout world of muckrakers
write with painstaking attempts to cajole reluctant filmmakers.
Monsanto chimes with food tampering that turns off most foodies
who are unaware of their terrorist support while chugging grape smoothies.
If the working class grew sensitive to the goods they fancy,

---

22   Upton Sinclair, writer whose novels argued for social reform

they would inspect their medicine cabinet, or inspect their pantries.
What if the general public realized that they are under hypnosis
that the media spoon-feeds propaganda in bite size doses?
Most name brand companies endorsed by favorite actors and actresses
are sealing deals with corrupt leaders administering illegal practices.
In 1984, government whistleblowers found Bayer® in connection
with selling blood clotting products that spread the HIV infection.
Of course, they curtailed its marketing plans to quell mass hysteria,
after dumping the contaminated items in Asia and Latin America.
Six thousand reported cases of ill Americans contracted the disease.
How long is the body count of the conglomerate's victims overseas?
Who reminded us "to never put bananas inside the refrigerator"?
Hint: they're the banana republic's[23] infamous terrorist instigator.
In 1928, **Chiquita®,** (then United Fruit Company), had an uprising
of Columbian workers that demanded better corporate compromising.
The army arrived pronto, set up their ammunition holsters,
and machine-gunned plantation workers holding up posters.
In 1954, the banana conglomerate staged a coup d'état
that resulted in a civil war, toppling Jorge Ubico of Guatemala.
The Department of Justice accused Chiquita of funding terrorist regimes.
to protect their plantations, aiding left wing and right wing extremes.
Outsourced pharmaceutical firms dumped various pollutants
into the world's drinking waters, transforming marine life to mutants.
Even US waters hold an undoubtedly high concentration
of pharmaceutical waste currently contaminating the nation.
Protest with passion as you must, pump your fist as you wish.
But be mindful of the social reform the people must accomplish.

---

23   Banana republic, a small nation, especially in Central America, dependent on one crop or the influx of foreign capital.

FAITH TESTED, LOVE APPROVED

Gathered at the round table were male divorcees
griping over a poker game about alimony fees.
I couldn't watch the moment erupt into malice and sadness,
so I tried to wax nostalgic over musical madness.
"Hey! Name three funk divas[24] affiliated with Prince
whose careers dissolved from then on since?"
They just jeered at me as if I was nuts.
These iTuners probably never heard of twelve inch cuts.
Never heard of Apollonia, Sheena Easton, Vanity;
all swept in a maelstrom of celebrity calamity
They inquired instead about me and my wife,
and how I averted divorce this far in my life.
Sifting through my collection for some Steely Dan,
I mulled over the question, and so I began:

---

24   Vanity, Apollonia, Sheena Easton, Sheila E. Taja Seville, Wendy & Lisa etc. Irrelevant to the tale but hey!

"At the next poker meet" I stifled my laugh,
"besides, it's my turn to give young Nigel a bath."
After stretching my limbs from a long ride home,
my scatterbrained thoughts began to roam.
My lady used to thrill me with tie dye sarongs,
glistening ankle bracelets, spider web thongs.
but past dating travesties dissolved my trust,
so hiring a private eye was a definite must.
Being a sailor left ample room for temptation.
Plus her crocodile tears deserved a standing ovation.
Upon leaving one day to sail to the Netherlands,
I promised on my return we'd see Caribbean sands.
That Friday I spilled beer nuts and **Heineken**® at a poetry slam.
One week later I was on a freighter bound for Amsterdam.
While in the English Channel, I made a telephone call
to my hired snoop and shady lover before nightfall.
Then, after work, I chuckled with hastened breath
while I chatted in secrecy with the ship's chef.
With that sly look of his, he asked if I was ready
for some Pothead Meatballs and Baked Spaghetti.
Some chopped onions, Indian relish, not enough breadcrumbs
so we minced the Texas toast with our forefingers and thumbs.
Cream of mushroom soup, a pound of hamburger meat,
a heaving helping of marijuana made the recipe complete.
Cooked the devil's meat wads into the simmering casserole
after deep frying the portions for five minutes as a whole.
Of course I had cared less about the consequences
that one plate of Cloud Nine rendered over my senses.
A week later the freighter arrived promptly on her itinerary.
(which was uncanny given how pilot logistics vary).
Soon me and my motley seafaring committee
did our utmost to tour all ends of the city.

We caught the No. 10 tram leading to Centraal Station[25];
there we took turns snapping pics at our destination.
Ventured into the Rijks museum, spotted dozens of rows
of scantily clad whores behind sliding glass windows.
Peered into a shop that showcased Indonesian jewelry,
found the famous "Mexico City" and the Heineken Brewery!
The drizzling rainfall failed to annoy the crew one bit.
I nearly lost my voice laughing at one comedy skit
performed at Boom Chicago on the topic of infidelity
before it dawned on me: they were playing my melody.
"If I find out the mailman's a lover in disguise,
I'll offer him the finest of Peruvian neckties[26]!"
I muttered among my peers yet under my breath,
contemplating whether I'd choke my woman to death.
Slumped against my chair, allowing depression to develop,
the thought of losing my better half made my eyes well up.
Whose idea was it to invest the retirement fund?
Who aimed the taser that left the burglar stunned?
She defended my absence at all the family functions,
the funereal processions, and her corporate luncheons.
My hawkish ego sunk lower than a pheasant.
Did I even consider buying her a single present?
Ever since I launched into holy matrimony
I've always suspected my sweet tenderoni,
driving myself to the sheer ends of paranoia
when I should have stood firmer than a Cali sequoia.
Startling my friends, I hopped out of my chair,
and rushed out of the club as if I was fleeing despair.
Fumbling with my change, I fought myself not to refrain
from phoning the investigator in the drizzling rain.

---

25   Centraal Station, the largest railway station of Amsterdam, Netherlands
26   Peruvian necktie, Tony De Souza's trademark submission is a modified guillotine chokehold.

GOD SAVE THE WOLF

"Free me, you bastards, I demand my lawyer!"
Steel bars compel me into a state of paranoia.
Regardless of my fabled speed, stamina, and agility,
that alone won't help me escape this correctional facility.
The prosecution charged me with aggravated assault,
deceit, and homicide—but I deny any fault.
This "David" stands defiant in the wake of "Goliath"

so you can tell the press or whoever you're with
that B.B. Wolf[27] continues to plead the fifth.
Don't portray my life journey as a fabricated myth.
If you're not a reporter, never mind what you heard.
Allow me to explain how the matter occurred:
I was on parole the other month for outstanding behavior
but, truth be told, my mentor did me a favor.
Seymour Lamb, a hedge fund manager and freelance bookie
who kept me under his wing back when I was a rookie.
That was the same wing that landed me in prison.
It took me thirty months to regain my vision.
He requested that we meet at a private golf course
to discuss how we'll rattle the crime world by force.
I reluctantly agreed. I vowed to stay clean.
Either that or imprisonment until 2015.
Mr. Lamb came late. He was so obsessed
to match his plumed fedoras with his Argyle vest.
I wore my **Raiders**® cap, tipped to the side,
with a sequined gold tee that left me satisfied.
We placed a fat wager on the eighteenth hole
but I was hesitant to gamble since I was still on parole.
Now Mr. Lamb was a pest who thought he was funny,
asked why I whined over "monopoly money."
That incessant distraction cost me the game.
That bickering shyster shouldered all the blame,
pocketed all the cash, and dumped all the shame.
Being criminally minded, I would have done the same.
Either I plan to reconcile like good natured friends
or I return to the truck contemplating revenge.
An hour later I was sulking in the Mercedes rental

27   B.B.Wolf, as in the Big Bad Wolf

humming along to Coltrane's "In a Mood Sentimental"
when I spotted that heckler stumbling to his Lamborghini
after two Whisky Sours and an apple Martini.
His earlier distractions prompted my sole vendetta
to have him staring at the muzzle of that shiny Beretta.
Pledged for payback, I approached the daft punk
at close range, plugged him, and flung him into the trunk
like a Tarantino flick viewed at the two dollar theatre.
Would you guess who I was barbequing three hours later?
Mulling over a delicious dish of rotisserie lamb chops,
hoping the homicide's overlooked by the cops.
I hissed in silence until a remnant of brittle bone
dissolved my devilish laughter into a plaintive groan:
"I invite all creatures to a handsome reward
to pull out this bone from my throat!" I roared
Remember that washed up mascot for **Vlasic Pickles®?**
Traded his life savings for worn buffalo nickels?
That stork relieved me of my pathetic situation
but first performed that Groucho Marx impersonation,
told me to bow down on my knees and freeze,
and the retiree seized the bone with ease.
Mr. Vlasic requested his due in return.
I shot back, "Piss off, birdbrain, not my concern.
Into the jaws of B.B. Wolf you placed your head
and retrieved it safely without dying instead?
You have the brazen audacity to ask for more
than your worthless existence to settle the score?"
I sped off in the rental to wherever I'm headed
when I figured I'm hurting for premium unleaded.
I pulled into an **Exxon®** when I peered at the bus stop:

an hourglass slimmy[28] working on a blow pop.

I motioned her over, then I delivered my pitch:

The phantom rims and fixtures convinced her I was rich.

The wolf game I toss is never sex-related,

but the tone of my voice keeps the females sedated.

Her name's Scarlet but she's also known as "L'il Red."

Pulled her aside for a ride but she reluctantly said,

"Today I gave Grandma my solemn oath

to visit her bedside with a gift in Sugarloaf[29]."

After exchanging pleasantries she skated for the bus,

I wondered if Scarlet or L'il Red was worth the fuss.

No travesty in paying homage, but then I'd bet

no Granny gets a care package from Victoria's Secret.

So, with a full tank of gas, I drove on to pay this Grandma a visit,

shove her into a retreat, and make the evening exquisite.

I found the miserable cottage centered in the middle of nowhere

though I raked my mane to make sense of the entire affair:

I broke in. Felt foolish. To a sly caper unorthodox,

"Grandma" was a blow up doll with a lubricated box.

I winched, feeling dumber than a burlap sack of rocks

when I heard, "Why are you still wearing your socks?"

Lights dimmed. It was Red wearing night nurse attire.

And she was willing to tend to my heart's desire.

"Are you a chubby chaser?", she added, fixing her face in a frown.

The pigs said you huffed and puffed and blew their homes down."

Then we heard footsteps. "Oh my, my husband's home early!

I told him I had an appointment with my hairdresser Shirley!"

Grabbing my shoes and socks, I muttered to myself with a grunt,

"Whatever possessed you to park the truck out front?"

I sprung out of the cottage in a flash, needless to ask or wonder

---

28   Slimmy, a slim trim young beauty.

29   Sugarloaf, a fictional place.

why the breadwinner was jotting down my license plate number.
Scarlet told the jury that I broke in with the intent to rape her,
and I wished I made the effort to merely video tape her.
Never mind the missing lamb and the rancid DNA evidence
in the Mercedes that I tried to write off as Bengali incense.
Wise words of caution: Lament and torture are all you will gain
when you're bound for Crime Central on that Midnight Train.

GOING BACK TO THAILAND

Depending on the prim grace of the pilot's reflexes,
flight 781 was slated to land in Austin, Texas
at 12:49 PM. Still no sign of the promised jet.
Other Shifty Air[30] travelers were growing upset,
like that elderly woman who hadn't flatlined yet.
Couldn't imagine her delivering an idle threat,
brandishing her "Light my Lucky" cigarettes,
can stop a speeding bullet with her **Cartier**® bracelets.
I enjoy a bit of risk so I fly with Shifty:
and, despite the recession, tend to live thrifty.

---

30   Shifty Air, fictional airlines.

My crumpled boarding pass made an excellent coaster
for the grape **Fanta**® that drained my **Kenny Rogers Roaster**[31]®.
Judging by their heightened eye-wristwatch coordination,
more Shifty Air patrons voiced mounting frustration.
Whiny teens smacked on **Bubblicious**® like arrogant cows.
Fidgeting neckties continued to newspaper browse.
At 1:19. I won my third No. 2 pencil fight
against an eighth grader who couldn't stomach his spite.
The overhead blared, "On time. Departing flight to Bangkok"
Pictured myself queuing there, averting Shifty's gridlock.
It felt like a decade passed since I treaded Siamese soil
and lamented the aftermath of the tsunami turmoil.
And the State Department declared Thai travel inadvisable,
aside from the onset of the nation's beloved Songkran Festival,
an aged tradition that began with their ancient tribes
to wash away the past year's misfortune, omens and bad vibes
transformed into a nationwide super soaker grudge match
with mischievous misfits dousing whomever they could catch.
Naysayers perceive Thailand as downright degrading
on countless news reports of topless T-girls masquerading.
No supporting research on the country's subtle splendors:
consider James Bond Island[32]. Gracious hair braiding vendors.
Kickboxing exploits. Elephant trekking tours.
Spicy coconut-based cuisines. Crafty paramours.
The sheer volume of Thai culture is beyond my reach;
I prefer haggling with the merchants along Patong beach.
An airline superintendent prodded me in the ribs.
Caught unaware, I motioned a signal that said, "What gives?"
A Shifty attendant queried whether I'd forego the flight
for a free pass to guess where? A strong chance I might.

---

31   Kenny Rogers Roaster, chicken from a chain of restaurants founded in by country musician Kenny Rogers
32   James Bond Island, Ko Tapu, also known as *James Bond Island*.

HEARTACHE IN HINDUSTAN

Mounting terror assaults plague cities worldwide.
No nation goes unaffected, seeking justice by its side.
Within the Indian subcontinent, subsequent blasts
are becoming as commonplace as weather forecasts.
Attacks in Jaipur, Mumbai, and other countless raids
haven given way to law enforcement's perverse brigades.
As police lock horns with alleged terrorists,
the issue of properly identifying the culprits exists.
Following the arrest of SIMI[33] leader Safdar Nagori,

---

33 Student Islamic Movement of India. SIMI aims to "liberate India" from Western cultural influences and
    convert it into a Muslim society that lives according to Muslim code of conduct. This organization is

unfortunate victims unveil an horrific story.
Individuals with little or no SIMI affiliation
can be wrongly subjected to public humiliation
if the police connect them with an extremist movement.
This demoralizing witch hunt has shown no improvement.
These terror counter measures target a young community
of random individuals suddenly marked for scrutiny.
Take Naved, of whom the staff insist lacked a tendency
to voice dissenting views at the two-wheeler agency.
Yet local police detained him after a grueling rap session
of stark interrogations, insisting he sign a false confession.
Once released from jail, his supervisors, under stern discretion,
demanded a case diary while he underwent clinical depression.
They claimed they would call him to explain his grievance;
Naved has yet to hear from the company since.
Afzal was headed home from his mobile phone repair shop
when he was confronted on the curb by an off duty cop.
There he was booked, fined and detained under police custody.
This man held no record of misdemeanors, let alone a felony.
Sentenced without substantial evidence, well over eight months,
the judicial courts considered his family's pleas not once.
Article Twenty One of the Indian Constitution
should have offered Afzal and Naved a promising resolution,
guaranteeing to its citizens that all governmental action,
despite frustration, seek uncompromised, unbiased satisfaction.
But the stigma of cooperating with extremist thugs still lingers
longer than several volts sent to electrode-taped fingers,
longer than the wife giving birth prematurely over the stress
of her spouse enduring mental anguish due to police duress.

---

believed by many to be involved in terrorism.

HOT DOG, HOT DOG, HOT DIGGITY DOG!!!

I remember when it was ill-mannered to turn down food;
as a welcomed dinner guest, you kept your dislikes subdued,
held a considerate stance, a thoughtful attitude.
Any disruptive action taken on your behalf was still rude.
However, setting the clock back to my grade school years,
refusing to gobble my veggies was common among peers.
Had I explained to Mommy Dearest once my caloric intake
exceeded my junk food regimen, I'd get a tummy ache,

would she have conceded and set down the pepper steak
then proceeded to offer me another **Hostess**® cupcake?
Probably not. But how will I act the moment I'm the father?
Would I discipline the brat? Raise my voice? Even bother?
Given how I would tackle the situation, I make no apology;
provided I render some reverse psychology.
Dust off my paperback Silverstein's *Light in the Attic*,
and read the tale of "Hungry Mungry", the eating fanatic.
And explain to the tyke by eating right—right now.
Daddy will teach you how to gorge meals like a cash cow.
Isn't that exactly how Takeru Kobayashi[34], the lion hearted,
Nagano born, six-time hot dog eating champ, got started?
He debuted in 2001, devouring fifty hot dogs in twelve minutes
at Nathan's Coney Island, astounding all doubtful critics.
Four years later, he appeared at the **Alka-Seltzer**® US Open,
bolted one hundred pork buns in twelve minutes shown on ESPN.
But with a dose of hilarity the Fox Network had the nerve to air
Man vs. Beast, where Kobayashi challenged a Kodiak bear.
Shattered Sonya Thomas's record in Sheboygan, Wisconsin,
by downing fifty-eight bratwurst sausages to seal his win.
I assume you'd gaze at me with an air of disgust
but, to entice my child into veggies, I will do as I must.
Kobayashi's a fine model for all mild eating disorders…
either that or find Piaget[35] at your nearby **Borders**®.

---

34   Takeru Kobayashi, set his first record at his rookie appearance when he ate 50 hot dogs in 12 minutes
35   Jean Piaget, Jean Piaget, a Swiss developmental psychologist and philosopher known for his
       epistemological studies with children.

IT'S ABOUT TO GO DOWN

Coasting along Highway 75, I made a blissful pause
to encounter a venue that benefited my cause:
The girlfriend and I split on less than graceful terms,
and I needed some refuge to assuage my nerves,
So I spun the Sentra into the Serenity Massage
located five blocks south of the **Econo Lodge**®.
I was quickly ushered in after ringing the bell
by a stunning masseuse waiting by the stairwell,
introducing herself to yours truly as Alanis Michelle,
before being welcomed as their favored clientele.
"We forged a joint merger with **Bath & Body Works**®

so, to our endearing guests, we offer the following perks:
In January, Serenity features aromatic therapy promotion
of olive oil, calamine and goat milk lotion.
Our theme-styled rooms match our finest ladies.
You can select from heaven, purgatory, or hades!"
Making my selection, I followed my escort
as she sashayed down the hall like an indoor sport.
I disrobed, showered, powdered in all discreet places
before slipping into this extravagant oasis.
Clad in Serenity shorts, I nosedived to the massage bed,
supine, relaxed from the neck down, adjusted my head,
Embarrassed--since right before the therapy starts,
I inadvertently launched one of those popcorn farts.
She averted her eyes to the coffee maker and found it unplugged
before noting my sheepish grin, my shoulders shrugged.
Wrinkling her nose, she passed me the Dallas Sun paper;
after peeling through the blurbs, I spotted the following caper:
One ranch owner's heart was torn asunder,
still reeling from the loss of his canine wonder.
"Skidboot", an Australian blue heeler, with a dog gone legacy
spanning over fourteen years with Dave Hartwig's chemistry.
A once famed showstopper at the Texas State Fair,
Thirty-eight states later, the jet setter's featured everywhere.
Spent an afternoon with Oprah, spent a late night with Letterman,
even tolerated Jay Leno! Skidboot was a veteran.
Once overcome by blindness, the cur's health deteriorated,
this sad dilemma alone left Hartwig frustrated.
Now Skidboot rests in peace, under convening oak trees
may his paw prints foster new canine legacies.
I wouldn't dare second guess that blue heeler's loyalty
anymore than Kobain's remorse for pennyroyal tea.
As for smoking hot beverages, tea or coffee's fine

provided, of course, there's no spit in mine.

Preferably from a coffee maker furnished by Madoff's Securities

whose ruthless brew filters all but Ponzi scheme impurities.

Bernard Madoff's fall generated a wide array of keepsakes:

his imprint on hair curlers, boomerangs, rattlesnakes .

Eventually, the sellers will sponsor a final sweepstakes

distributed on eBay for all unscrupulous flakes.

Tickled by the essay and the masseuse's fingernails,

sliding up past my calves along with her pigtails,

With a glance, I bid my magician good bye

after an exhilarating massage from neck to thigh.

Then, with my muscles limber, my empathy riper,

I proceeded to the counter to pay the piper.

Once money exchanged hands, I was out and about,

enhanced in ways few can do without!

52

JAPANESE HORROR

Ever wonder how "amped up" movie aficionados muster
their inner courage to accept the end of Blockbuster?
I used to head to the avant garde aisle, all by myself,
rummaging through the Tartan indie films scattered over the shelf,
sifting for a subtitled version of Takashi Miike's[36] Ichi the Killer.
The last time I'd choose the slasher theme over the psychological thriller.
I admit feeling bitter over the young upstart Red Box snub
that singlehandedly dismantled America's favorite rent-a-flick hub,
even though it failed to dull cinema passion, or managed to rub

---

36   Takashi Miike, a highly prolific and controversial Japanese filmmaker.

off much on moviegoers with an Alamo ticket stub.
Don't get me misconstrued with avid moviegoers.
I don't recall Mad Max toting M2 flamethrowers.
Forget quipping lines from "the 40 year old Virgin."
Forget waxing poetic about the movie "Time Surgeon".
Rather, get drunk in a roach motel with Charles Milles Manson
than cuddle for two hours to the iconic "Dirty Dancing"
You wouldn't? Until now, I've evaded many a chick flick.
That's why I'm single, home alone, serenading my d____.
I'm quite content ditching circles spewing that cinematic fluff
I'm not a movie buff in any sense of the word—enough!
But I'm unable to foresee the day when I say, "Sayonara"
to my unrequited love with the world of J-horror.
"Uzumaki", (or aptly titled in the West as "Spiral").
would cause me to "fall out" if this motion picture ever went viral.
Ito manga turned film, staged in a small town
where the lead character's father is a swirl-obsessed clown.
Unlike your usual action packed theme that places emphasis
on pairing the protagonist with the dark stark nemesis,
"Uzumaki" centers on the existing phenomenon in nature
overwhelming a village with psychedelic behavior.
Enter "Battle Royale", then contemporary "Hunger Games"
or "Lord of the Flies". Different eras. Different names.
A cult classic. Forty-two bratty middle schoolers
found their time off far unbelievable than Ferris Bueller's.
Three days to determine who will victor in the fight for survival
with the insight of learning which best friend will turn rival.
However, the premise of the film remained unclear
to me, at least. But the B list movies I do hold dear
are the original "Grudge" and the prequel to the "Ring"
devoid of splatter punk, so much is happening.
I'm aware that most enthusiasts are less than willing

to admit that the best character was in fact the villain.
One reviewer described "Ring O" as a Shakespearean tragedy
whereas "Juon's" director set vengeful spirits on a killing spree.
Sadako, in "The Ring", embodied a veil of fabled mystique:
her mother fornicated with the sea and produced a freak.
Juon hinted to viewers that one salaryman's housewife
committed adultery, and eventually lost her life.
"When a woman is full of resentment, she will bring frost in May and June."
After watching these pictures, it's difficult to assume
which consequence came first, last or whether it mattered.
One thing is certain: The precept of horror had been shattered.
Tales of the macabre without harboring any detailed bloodshed
still captivated the pangs of the hungry audience instead.
I'm far more disgruntled with the American rendition,
wishing their snake oil remedies never came to fruition.
Producers had to dilute the genre of the foreign trendsetter.
Did Sarah Michelle Gellar make "The Grudge" that much better?
You bet I'm biased! And I do not sympathize with investors' throes.
Let them make their fast buck based around comic book heroes.
As of late, my motion picture interests have shifted to non-existent.
My aversion to pop culture presentations is that persistent.
Not to infer that Japanese horror failed to recapture
my zeal; it's time to turn the page, and start a new chapter.

JOURNALIST'S CODE OF ETHICS

There appears to be a lack of integrity in the media nowadays.
Even long running publications have joined in on the craze.
The late essayist Andy Rooney wrote a code of ethics refined
into a few statements from his book entitled, *Pieces of My Mind.*
The public decides the truth. Journalists report the facts;
report the facts regardless of how the public reacts;
report the facts regardless of whomever it attacks;
report the facts regardless of whether it warrants drawbacks.
Once the journalist grabs ahold of the public's ear,
they tell what they ought to know, never what they want to hear.
Acts of brownnosing or sweet hearting of all sorts

should be kindly dismissed when delivering one's reports.
The journalist mustn't yield or buckle to higher forces
on grounds he or she confided not to reveal their sources.
Never attempt to use their profession to espouse any cause
despite its apparent merits and upholding bylaws.
A rough estimate of his statements compromised in rhyme
but, in the blogosphere, dishonesty is a dismissive crime.
Hold bloggers responsible for their written words;
what the message entails, denotes, and what it infers.
Monitor blog remarks with utmost discretion.
Halt abusive comments instilling heavy aggression.
Media writers react to such proposals with strong disdain,
and feel opening doors to censorship would be downright insane.
Apparently, most online yellow journalists would self-destruct
if the blogging world fell prone to a code of conduct.

LOVE IS DEAF, DUMB AND BLIND

Classes ended at three. I was on the brink to unload
a full day's lecture until tomorrow's episode.
I raced for the bus bound for Rockville station;
aside from antsy to get home, no particular occasion.
Jansport® duffle bag smacking behind my back.
Sony Discman® chopping the vocals of Roberta Flack.
The **Metrobus**® dropped off a smiling passenger
who eyed me as if predicting the worst to occur.
While reading "watch your step" I tripped onto the bus,
but that was nothing to the outrage I seldom discuss.
My first step was my last. And I couldn't lean back.

Caught in my face were tattered jeans and plumber's crack.
To my left sat a short, wiry, mentally challenged lady
who started caressing my arm like a newborn baby.
Unable to wrest my arm free, I resisted the urge
to scream at my sweetheart as if I lacked the courage.
Either I signal the driver to make the next stop.
or stomach the humility as a freak show prop.
The laughter ensued. The woman started humming.
No doubt in mind what was finally coming.
The driver dropped hints, halting at each destination,
no doubt hoping to aid me in finding salvation.
When I departed I refrained from a causing a fuss,
I smirked at the new sucker ready to board the bus!

MASS HYSTERIA. JUST IN TIME FOR THE HOLIDAYS

Last night I was hammered at the Absinthe Café
contemplating a lusty nightcap with a bottle of Alizé;
but I diversify, you crumbs, ask my mixologist
who's delivered more souls than John the Baptist.
I took seven Martinis, put them in a line,
added seven shot glasses of Japanese plum wine.
Well it'll take seven more before I drink and drive,
so I stay sh!tfaced on Fridays until half past five.
This piece I dedicate to the morning-breath lovers,
sloppy seconds is a great excuse to stay under the covers.

But I swear I just choked on a swallow of spit
from this sixteen ounce of canned coffee. Who's the culprit?
Now wasn't the moment to offer any saliva,
but no one else is present save Lady Godiva
watching the latest episode of Bridezilla;
must have been an invisible java sipping gorilla.
Mentioning guerilla, several gun men left
one hundred eighty eight victims preoccupied with death
in Mumbai last November, injuring over three hundred;
now India awaits to see justice fed.
But how would you interpret unlamented mob rage?
In the wake of Black Friday, **Walmart**® set the stage.
In their vehement hunt for low prices, one crowd went berserk,
smashed the front doors, and flattened a clerk.
Although the man died from one of the most incredulous fates,
not one Samaritan rose from the herd of cheapskates.
Pronounced dead in an hour, as police reports stated,
I hope that his loved ones were properly compensated.
Do mass murderers backed by political members
outweigh a stampeding mob armed with legal tenders?
Although I've grown thick-skinned to the outrage society does,
leave it to **CNN**® to upset my morning buzz.

MOON RIVER

Yeah, the name's Holly[37]. Did I ask you yours?
I didn't. Don't compare me with these arrogant bores.
Let's make a deal. Since I'm holding on to my final cigarette,
I'll trade you: My life story for a butt to square off the debt.
Buenos Aires, Argentina was my home away from home,
pending litigations compelled me forever to roam.
One balmy evening, I was sipping a Mimosa,
ladies night, Club 69, by the Zona Rosa,
where I met Salvador Allende[38]—that's my Sally

---

37   Holly Golighty. the main character of Truman Capote's novella Breakfast at Tiffany's.
38   Salvador Allende, first Marxist to become president of a Latin American country

(like my Sally Tomato but from Paradise Valley).
When it comes to men, call me Ms. Meticulous:
picky, picky, picky to the point it's ridiculous.
But Sally could tango like Rudolph Valentino,
entertain me with glances over cups of cappuccino,
urging me to accompany him back to his palace,
guaranteeing a return ticket at the slight hint of malice.
Then, with a hop, skip, and a seven-hundred mile jump,
his Cessna arrived with a deafening thump.
Santiago was amazing, just as he said:
La Moneda, Sculpture Park, but soon it led
to a sad day of infamy since his very opponent
was General Pinochet, I'll explain in a moment.
Just let me grab a quick toke of that Marlboro.
My two pack limit used to keep me thorough.
Dear Sally was an elected government official
in Chile, but his victory proved a disturbing issue
to Nixon, prompting a major propaganda campaign
to secure American interests for capital gain.
When that failed, the CIA abetted a coup d'etat.
One day while entertaining his guests with mock baccarat,
I was still mesmerized by Allende's pillow talk;
Pinochet threatened to outline his body in chalk.
Next, I caught Sally hammering the wall,
collapsing and, convulsing before attempting to crawl.
The chaos left my heart slumped in regret;
that day of those "mean reds" I swore to never forget
It's the day Santiago crumbled to its own 9/11[39]
It's the day Allende left en route to heaven.
It's the day Augusto Pinochet expressed his scorn

---

39 Chile's 9/11, The 1973 **Chilean** coup d'état was a watershed event in the Cold War.

with Hawker Hunter fighter jets sent airborne
driving missiles into la Moneda, the presidential palace.
My love addressed the nation, with precise callous.
Again collapsing, his hands raked about in the bedroom parlor
for a Soviet-issued automatic problem solver.
One bodyguard and a maid found Sally sunk
in a guest room brewing in machine gun funk.
Either by grace or sheer fate, dignitaries turned friends
escorted me, in secret, into a dilapidated Benz,
bypassing tanks and rifleman of the emerging junta,
onward to Buenos Aires over semi-paved tundra.
Once in Argentina, I decided to court
my phony identity and counterfeit passport,
and fly coach back to the infamous New York City
to seek redemption with an AA committee.
Instead I am wasting away again in Margarita Ville,
Sipping Cadillac Margaritas with lime, but still
I strum Moon River on my way to **Tiffany's®**,
withering away in my jaded fantasies.

MR. CHI-CITY

Never have I seen another talent pour his heart into a vlog,
mustering a flippant approach to a witty monologue
than YouTube personality, the one and only Mr. Chi-city.
He even launched a tirade at the YouTube committee.
Yet one video he posted resembled a Shakespearean tragedy.
Although I'm exaggerating the affair, it was a definite must-see.
We tagged along with our crusader on a snow-laden road
leading to a cemetery and felt his heart explode,
while he remained light-hearted as he made his confession

of how his friend's girlfriend was engulfed in deep depression.

Chi-city admitted having to endure his own bouts of denial.

How the loss of his companion became a plaintive trial.

Although his intimate presentation remains in modest rotation,

you ought to view the video that made him a YouTube sensation.

Here's my disclaimer: I must offer this spoiler alert ahead.

He reveals how to stock the refrigerator to lure a woman to bed.

A bachelorette's behavior is determined by the beverage she drinks

based on the conducive atmosphere, or at least that's how he thinks.

Fitness buffs rejuvenate their figures on **Vitamin Water**®

whereas single mothers need freeze pops for their son or daughter.

Hood chicks prefer **Kool-Aid**®, or upgrade to **Cherry Coke**®.

That calorie intake is not enough to induce a minor stroke.

Siddity urban chicks brake for the tall boy **Arizona**® ice teas.

Snapple® quenches the thirst of high life suburban "Becky's."

MILFs moan for **Mystic**®; green tea or water for holistic vegetarians.

Pantry stocked with "snacks on snacks" for vicarious barbarians.

Chi-city tends to woo his audience with the mundane objects at home;

for instance, his "Italian" tile work or his wastebasket made of chrome.

In another video, he exchanged heated discourse with his cable service

to the extent that our exhausted hero grew more and more nervous.

He explained that the dilemma affected his sex life,

assuming Donahue[40] couldn't be reached to examine his strife.

Mr. Chi-city garnered swelling accolades of Internet support

for fighting a vehicular violation on his day in traffic court.

Honestly, there's more value to his work than I can provide.

so I suggest you tune in to YouTube, and brace yourself for the ride.

---

40   Phil Donahue, is an American media personality, writer, and film producer best known as the creator and host of *The Phil Donahue Show.*

NEVER FORGET: 9–12

It was roughly one in the morn. Another starry night in Guam[41].
With dampened sleeves, I smeared sweat into the small of my palm.
Figured from the Ichiban hotel I'd roll into Lower Tumon,
hit the **Hard Rock®**, catch a buzz, sleep away the afternoon.
But first I bought some macadamias from the ABC Market.
So what prompted that man to mark me as a target?
That man in the off-white Chevy van offered me a ride
to the naval base, insisting he'd make room inside.

---

41   Guam, an organized, unincorporated territory of the United States.

I fired that was unnecessary. Me? Intoxicated?
Plus no service man was bound to get me frustrated.
He cut it short. Told me that the Twin Towers were struck
by passenger jets, the outrage sent the Big Apple running amok.
I was in shock. His intelligence from the US was spot on
and soon, hours later, the whole island caught on.
The military poised to mobilize all forces in ninety-six hours:
ready to rain on our foes with indiscriminate lead showers.
But the energy was odd. Guam's far too remote an area
to grasp the mainland's strangle hold of hysteria.
Not to imply that she criticized Manhattan's heroics.
In fact she held a candlelight vigil for the city of stoics.
However, a fifteen hour time difference did more to defuse
the island-wide uproar than the dated coverage of the news.
Each day ran its course with unvarying ease
except nobody felt obliged to inform the Japanese.
Sixty percent of Guam's economy relied on the tourist yen.
Yet not one infomerical channel made room for anchormen.
The thriving downtown area turned ghost town overnight:
vacant trolleys, deserted beaches: not a lurker in sight.
Alleged weekend excursions lasted for days on end.
Air carriers consoled passengers during the downtrend.
My intention is not to garner any false pretense;
only one perspective warranted from my experience.
Only my reflection on the matter unknown to most
fellow Americans living on either side of the coast.

PANHANDLING SCAMMERS

One night I dreamt that Latoya Jackson wanted me to get on
the dial-a-psychic network as she incessantly waved her baton.
With a finger wagging gesture, I motioned her to the **Tiger Balm®**,
Those vagabonds aren't expecting me to read their palm;
Hot eucalyptus oil penetrated my upper back and forearms
with enough iron-smelting heat to melt smoke alarms.
I woke up sweating and stirring at the **Golden Gate Doubletree®**,
second guessing my itinerary over what I should see.
I swear I was accosted by legions of clean-shaven deadbeats
the moment I wandered through Chinatown in search of cheap eats.

San Francisco's teeming with derelicts loitering on every corner;
albeit some were cable guys being laid off by **Time Warner**®.
But the ruse is so phony—God knows it's beyond obvious
that any sap who gives should be advised to stay anonymous.
The **United Way**® may have had an unnerving history
of misallocating funds meant for muscular dystrophy,
granted, but their path is earmarked with the best of intentions.
Unlike these day to day hustlers of whom no one questions.
They approach me when they're scrounging for bus fare.
One speech major bragged about his earnings while spinning a wheelchair.
But I am among the suspicious few who consider it funny
that the best charities bid your time instead of money.
Sometimes, government legalese hinders soup kitchen ambitions
yet Toys For Tots and turkey drives are still prided traditions.
So veer closer to the street and ensure your hard earned dime isn't spent
Your contribution won't cure their arrested development.

POLE POSITION

I tried my utmost to decipher the last leg of the dream:
I treaded lava like gondolas, cascading downstream
toward the mouth of the bay, hissing bubbles around me
in that grotto of mist, not a soul would have found me
except those faceless cadavers drowning below.
After brushing this creature from the magma flow,
its two emerging arms wrestled me, with the skill of a python,
unyielding, in the grip of a daemon liaison.
The motive of my captor left me befuddled,
brooding whether I was being tackled or cuddled.

My eyes flashed open to a persistent clock
yet failed to bring an end to the lurid shock.
The sensation lasted seconds later, despite hampered reflexes,
before I began a late morning in breezy Texas.
Must be that espresso anxiety inherited from my father.
Those sirloins are nesting at 350 degrees so don't bother.
And as for those potatoes, leave it to the pantry genie;
all for the sacrifice of one dry Martini.
I know you don't drink—still— polite to ask.
(I know you've been dying all night to ask.)
Since Loyola's offering, she can have whatever she wants.
Were you hoping I'd deliver some heated response?
The term's "pole fitness", no longer "pole dancing."
and it's the sweeping trend from Lafayette to Lansing.
Weren't you, at one time, the aerobics enthusiast?
How is this different from your typical gymnast?
Their trainer insists their heads down and bums up?
That's the sole reason I gave her the thumbs up!
But seriously, you're aware that what comes up,
must come down. Consider how often her ego numbs up.
What impressionable acts did you think this course would bestow?
Men sopping fountains of red wine streaming down her left toe?
If it's not that so what frustrates you then?
That it appeals to women? That it appeals to men?
I presume "the revolution will not be panty lined"[42]
now that the feminist movement comes to mind.
Your brand of ideologies have long since died,
with burning Thatcher effigies, resetting feminist pride.
We're not ones to judge, so let's give her the chance
to follow her instincts or rethink the circumstance.

---

42   The movement... a pun on the poem entitled "The Revolution Will Not Be Televised" is a poem and
      song by Gil Scott-Heron.

PUBLIC BUS HASSLES

I box my ears whenever snobs discuss
their tear-jerking experiences of riding the bus.
I've earned my stripes along the lines of public transit,
And I don't take the concrete jungle for granite.
But taking the bumble bee bus to school as a kid
meant conflicting results for whatever you did.
Bullies and hecklers usually in the sat in the back
taunting the younger kids with the same attack:
cursing, slapping their ears or having spitball fights,
and pencil fights before an instigated brawl ignites.

The driver would threaten to stop the bus
when the eighth graders got too rambunctious.
Tensions eased when you became the older kid
until then the coveted front row is where you hid.
Walkmans hinted that students wanted to be left alone.
Boom boxes meant blaring music on the ride home.
At least in those days your classmates joined you;
while public transit passengers struggle to avoid you,
dodging pasty worn seats tiptoeing over food crumbs
in hopes of claiming a chair away from the back seat bums.
Usually, it's the senior citizens that talk you to death,
rambling on about the past without losing a breath.
The bus provides plenty game for a pick up artist;
an inauspicious place for a fledging stick up artist.
Women sense your motives once the bus enters,
pulling up into any one of those transit centers.
CCTV, unnoticed, makes thieves ease their guard
when they're out mugging marks for their debit card.
Sometimes a violent exchange on the public bus ensues,
Youtube® gets the footage, spurring a million views.
One instance known as "the AC Transit Bus Fight"
where the "Epic Beard Man" pummeled a man outright.
Having a bad day, Michael Lovette was met with flurries
of heavy handed punches resulting into facial injuries.
While Michael Lovette and Thomas Bruno weren't arrested,.
their feedback on the confrontation was duly requested.
In another incident following the widely viewed altercation,
Thomas Bruno was hospitalized for a mental evaluation.
It's best to drive a simple lemon than dealing with a fuss
which can be easily averted by avoiding the public bus.

REBATING YOU IN A CIRCLE JERK

I rode the money back guaranteed rebate wave in 2003
before **Cingular**® rebranded itself as **AT&T**®.
Customer feedback then was not at all unnerved.
Their devotion to the clients was a title well deserved.
Cingular honored every rebate and offered no question.
In fact, I convinced my brothers to join my new obsession.
Then AT&T returned. I grimaced, unable to cope with the scrimmage.
Cingular Wireless was a decoy to jumpstart **Bell South's**® image.
My eye opener to shifty store tactics began in Hong Kong
where a deal in owning a gadget had gone wrong.

After waiting patiently, my mission went stale

once told the device was no longer on sale.

But his sales pitch goaded me to consider another item.

Felt like Rose Royce was singing "Déjà vu". ad infinitum[43].

The player was fantastic. No excuse to whine or bitch

until I realized I was targeted for the bait and switch.

I admit that wasn't rebate related. Still a work in progress.

If you sense the same plot you mustn't second guess.

I'll seek Bob Sullivan to aid me in regaining my tempo

from his work Gotcha Capitalism concerning Marie Vento.

Looking back on 2005, **Razr**® mobiles were the hipster's rage.

Their ubiquitous design emerged in cyber ads via pop-up page

with a money back guarantee. Who wouldn't indulge?

Six months later she incited her version of the Battle of the Bulge[44].

Vento, stunned to receive a rejection notice

due to an "invoice bill date" redoubled her focus.

Processing centers gave the New Yorker the run around;

the labyrinth of red tape is what ran her ship aground.

The shortest path to consumer justice is the Better Business Bureau.

Either that or resign yourself to the works of Henry Thoreau[45].

Ebenezer Scrooge, in hindsight, had the practical attitude

for money affairs, although depicted as an absolute crude.

Do your due diligence. It's your money. You do your homework.

Thus, lessen the chances of Main Street driving you berserk.

---

43   Ad infinitum meaning "to infinity" or "forevermore".

44   Battle of the Bulge, was a major German offensive campaign launched through the densely
      forested Ardennes region of Wallonia in Belgium, France, andLuxembourg on the Western Front toward
      the end of World War II

45   Henry Thoreau anAmerican author, poet, philosopher, abolitionist, naturalist, tax resister, development
      critic, surveyor, and historian.

RETIREMENT ISSUES

Congratulations on the seminar! You really pulled it off!
You claimed more ears than Mike Tyson bit off.
And those cynics at the firm insisted you were bound to bomb
as a get-together trendsetter using meetup dot com.
You reassured our guests that uttering the four letter word
"S-A-V-E" at holiday spending events is hardly absurd.
Making reservations at El Chico was an elegant touch,
considering me and the missus seldom dine out as much.
Before you plunge your fork into that smokehouse fajita,
and lap up the salt off of that Cadillac Margarita,
let's review the presentation with the *Sullivan*[46] manual.
Now that the smoke has cleared we can act more casual.

---

46   Sullivan manual, rather the book entitled Gotcha Capitalism.

Common buzzwords used today regarding retirement
are 401ks and stable IRAs as the Main Street requirement.
But it requires more than a light hearted approach
when dealing with the guiles of a Wall Street roach.
Agencies take their doomsday reference on consumer spending
with statistics displaying saving habits down trending.
Taking a cue from observing the disappointed looks,
they suggest the public burn their Suzie Orman books.
But, in the case of 401ks, agents won't lisp a word
about the line item "expense ratios" fees incurred.
Expense ratios peak from 0.25 percent to 2 percent,
exclusive to the firms that deal with money management.
Studies reveal that even a 1 percent charge, given twenty years,
means a 17 percent claim in retirement funds disappears.
Sadly, the "k" in "401k" is a euphemism for kickbacks.
Funny how Main Street is double-crossed with railroad tracks.
Fund managers insure you incur second degree financial burns
in the name of compounding costs on your invested returns.
Some companies select third party contractors slated to draft
"revenue sharing" guidelines on the worker's behalf.
But those administrations involved make themselves richer.
Even the money-savvy overlook the negatives and fail to see the picture.
Consult the human resource department on expense ratios,
revenue sharing, and other hidden fees regarding money portfolios.
Avoid company stocks with carrot-baiting thrifty fees,
or at least contribute 10 percent— tops— despite their policies.
Clients should feel entitled to wage wars with institutions
given their survival relies on paid worker's contributions.
Stomp out the money grubbing Wall Street cucaracha.
Fight back or fall prone to the corporate gotcha!

SINO–AUSSIE RELATIONS ON RUDD'S WATCH

No nation greatly profited from China's industrial thunder
until the last fiscal year than the "Land Down Under".
China's coal and iron demands kept traders churning,
manufacturers developing, and politicians returning
to engage in diplomatic and economic stimulus talks
while the disapproving populace of their relations balks.
Last November, Beijing announced that it would pump
Four trillion yuan into the world market despite the slump.

Although China makes Australia's prime export market,
swelling empathy towards Tibet makes China a viral target.
Prime Minister Kevin Rudd[47] ponders whether security measures
be implemented in response to Beijing's hostile endeavors.
An influx of Chinese firms, amid the financial crisis,
sought to usurp Australian raw mineral enterprises
in response to plummeting shares and commodity prices.
Canberra's done little to defend mining sacrifices.
Political pundits stand divided on Sino-Australian relations
since the prime minister left them embarrassed on scant occasions:
Liberal Party's John Howard looked on to his utmost chagrin
while Rudd addressed Chinese diplomats in fluent Mandarin.
Although there's no real harm to flushing egos aside,
the Great Dragon shouldn't tamper with a nation's pride.
In 2008 Rudd watched in Canberra, with a degree of patience,
Chinese brass drill students on stifling Tibetan demonstrations.
A blemish in the armor of the Australian community,
strutting oppression on foreign soil without fear of impunity.
Aside from Tibet, Rudd juggles wavering Taiwanese sentiment,
surging mining development, and growing public dissent.
Should Canberra continue to cater to Beijing's interests
due to upward flow in mining exploits where China invests?
Should zoo workers and authorities deliver memorandas
to disallow koala bears from politicking with pandas?
While Australia works hard to balance its diplomatic elixir,
onlookers hope the US prolongs its stay in the regional picture.

---

47 Kevin Rudd a former Australian politician who was twice Prime Minister of Australia serving from 2007 to 2010 and again from 27 June 2013 to 18 September 2013.

SLEEPING WITH THE ENEMY

So many tales of betrayal flood the pages of the Bible.
It's safe to conclude that treachery was the means of survival.
Scripture dictates that humans must love their sister and brother,
but I haven't found a verse implying we should trust each other.
If it weren't the religious texts depicting the plight of Elijah,
I'd assume most tragedies resembled Samson and Delilah.
Due to naked vulnerabilities, who wants to uncover
the calculated deception of a jilted lover?
I have compassion for the star-studded figures in the public eye.
Celebrities hemorrhage as their reputations die.

I cringed when the gossip hounds at TMZ were unfurling
the controversies regarding Mel Gibson and Donald Sterling.
People magazine hailed Gibson as the "Sexiest Man Alive"
two years prior to the "Mad Max" films in 1985.
The Lethal Weapon actor separated from his loyal wife of twenty-six years
with a settlement that would have cast Hulk Hogan into tears.
His then mistress released an audio message on the Internet
that hurled the Apocalypto filmmaker into a cold sweat.
Although Gibson apologized for launching racial epithets
at his three year old's mother along with incisive threats,
his racist, sexist and anti-Semitic remarks altogether
prompted his release from his agency, "William Morris Endeavor."
While Civil Rights leaders called for a boycott of Gibson's pictures,
the ordeal totaled nearly a million dollars in joint custody expenditures.
Donald Sterling was removed as the owner of a professional basketball team
due to a recorded conversation that sent his integrity downstream.
According to the controversial recording, TMZ Sports affirms
Sterling approved his female friend dating blacks under discreet terms.
That caveat meant not to bring her male friends to the games,
the implication reduced the LA Clippers to dribbling lames.
The embarrassing scandal set the federation in flames.
The heartfelt reaction was summed up best by Lebron James:
"There's no room for Donald Sterling in the NBA."
Players wore reversed jerseys in protest of Sterling's foul play.
Then Sterling sued V. Stiviano, his acquaintance and paramour,
and his estranged wife acted likewise to settle the score.
NAACP then canceled Sterling's lifetime achievement prize.
The NBA chairman moved that the Lakers owner forfeit the franchise.
Why should the invasion of privacy of taxpaying civilians
receive duress due to the public opinion of millions?
Granted, this form of entrapment doesn't warrant a felony,
but to violate one's trust for spite is a moral travesty.

SNEAKER WONDERLAND

Fashionistas in my circle would find it absurd
to bill me a sneakerhead in any sense of the word.
So no one would expect me to blurt out, or mention,
a word about Houston's Annual Sneaker Convention.
Kids teased me in school for sporting no name kicks
longer than jheri curl relaxers replaced afro picks.
I remember the days when devoted sneaker aficionados
canceled orders on **Diadoras**® but held out for **Lotto's**®.
Fila®. **Ellese**®. **K-swiss**®. **Bally**®. **British Knights**®.
Jordan's® got you shot, strangled, or embroiled in fights.
A vigil for the unsuspecting few that wound up dead
for mistaking a sneaker fiend for a sneaker head.

A sneaker fiend's credit is smeared with unpaid debts.
A sneaker fiend's home is filled with starving pets.
A sneaker fiend's cigs and blunts pepper **Champs**® outlets.
A real sneaker fiend harbors no regrets.
To gather an understanding of the footwear craze,
we must set the time capsule towards the "Thriller" days,
earmarking the debut of basketball's iconic shoe:
Nike® released the "Air Force One's" in 1982.
Aside from its technology, it offered an opportunity
to set new trends and designs in the urban community.
For instance, an agile break-dancer, on a day-to-day basis,
would spice up their **New Balance**® with two-toned fat laces.
Ever since strategic manufacturers constantly came up
with rap celebrities insisting you step your shoe game up.
One day the trend that emerged from the basketball courts
will find its way to speculators through NASDAQ reports.
Sneaker enthusiasts will head to Houston's NGR Center.
Quarter to two, for parking's sake, is the best time to enter.
Showcasing Turntablists, Athletes, Streetwear Designers
selling CDs, autographs, raffles for Caribbean ocean liners.
They'll be tens of thousands of preying sneaker summit attendees!
Don't wait too late to order at your local participating **Wendy's**®.

SNL KOREA®

I once concluded that the late night sitcom lost its relevance;
a mere caricature of its heyday to the viewing audience.
Despite my hiatus from the program, I must confess;
that "Enemy of the State" skit was straight hilarious.
When gossiping about divas, don't compromise yourself;
bad-mouthing Beyoncé can be hazardous to your health.
That "Justin Timberlake" sketch was a yuletide classic,
even though the show's sponsors had reason to panic.
I enjoyed the obnoxious antics of late comedian, Gilda Radner,
and the Dennis Miller interview with Marvelous Marvin Hagler.
Steve Martin and Dan Aykroyd were "two wild and crazy guys."
Now the sitcom's turned forty without a sign of demise.
But wouldn't you rather stay up in your plaid pajamas,

remote in hand, and watch Nickelodeon dramas?
I remember a time when the cast was suffering
with lackluster talents snorting lines of **"Bufferin®"**.
As a pre-teen I realized SNL wasn't worth creeping
late to watch the guest band perform; I was better off sleeping.
Although some members left to make awesome movies,
I was disinterested until I heard about their ventures overseas.
Imagine: "Live from Seoul it's Saturday Night!"
It'll take more than subtitles to freshen my appetite.
There's one wild sketch in which one mother speculates
that her bashful teenage son incessantly masturbates.
She learns how to condone it, as a doting mother should.
But he struggles to explain that she misunderstood;
because of haphazard situations he wishes he could,
but his dear mother convinced he's beating the wood.
I've enjoyed the spoofs entailing the computer game "Desperado"
that explores a zany spinoff of "Grand Theft Auto"...
One offshoot that thrilled me were the "SNL Digital Shorts"
or music videos performed by host Shin Don-yup and cohorts.
The lead writer *Jang Jin* manages to uphold the late night show identity
without sacrificing a smidgen of artistic integrity.
Cable broadcasting veers "SNL Korea" away from political traffic,
insensitive jokes pit them against their viewing demographic.
Overseas Koreans blasted the show for the orphan jokes,
claiming it insults the Diaspora[48], and the confusion it provokes.
Another skit was the rendition of "Dreamgirls" in blackface.
Suffice to write why that broadcast was an utter disgrace.
Amid their growing pains, I find "SNL Korea" amazing,
and I'm certain that the cast will continue trailblazing.

---

48   The **Korean diaspora** consists of roughly seven million people, both descendants of early emigrants from the Korean peninsula, as well as more recent emigres from Korea.

SOMETHING ABOUT A
GLASS OF ORANGE JUICE

Bargain hunters fancy themselves as being so clever
for toting a ton of coupons for their mighty **Walmart**® endeavor.
Unconvinced that impulsive shopping tempted them to dire sins
such as rummaging for hair gels in the bargain basement bins.
And how about that holier-than-thou gluten-free shopper
with IQ's higher than calories on a **Burger King Whopper**®?
Rant over. Why bother whining about supermarket abusers?
I'm really bent on purchasing a couple of **Breville**® juicers,
given that a glass of fruit juice should make you overly cautious;
filled with suspect chemicals that make children nauseous.
Ever wonder why orange juice is abundant throughout the year,
regardless of the season? No harvest too severe?
Those **Sunkist**® navels sitting in the fresh produce corridor
likely came from the juice mecca: Polk County, Florida.

Of course, I accrued that knowledge from the **Discovery**® channel,
explaining how all is maintained behind a dusty control panel.
One interesting tidbit was omitted from that ten minute episode:
like what preserves the juices from the fruits they unload.
Within state-of-art factories, what they precisely did
was pulp the orange, deaerate it, and store the liquid.
Not to mention pasteurizing methods that sapped its entire flavor!
Yet **Tropicana**® and **Minute Maid**® granted consumers one favor:
They added preservatives like "ethyl butyrate" and "xanthan gum"
to restore its sweetness and make your taste buds numb.
By tapping the shoulders of companies like **Christian Dior**®,
parent firms **Pepsi**® and **Coca Cola**® did their utmost to ensure
special "flavor packs" keep their products far from flaccid,
and threaten super sensitive teeth with citric acid.
Capitalism dictates the household shopper must be appeased.
Nonetheless, the muckraking author of the paperback, *Squeezed*,
Alissa Hamilton detailed the exploits in a Yale U publication
within her two hundred eighty eight page compilation.
Since no rotgut publishing is worth my twenty six dollars,
I have nothing to offer a litter of baby Rottweilers.
Tropicana redoubled their efforts to dispel rumors
of discrepancies that resulted in misleading consumers
in a suit action, insisted their firm stayed in compliance
of labeling laws and regulations supported by their clients.
Beverage behemoth Minute Maid would later denounce
overlooking fungicide carbendazim in trace amounts
from exporters when queried by FDA whistleblowers.
Another allegation to endure by committed orange growers.
Horton[49] hears an opportunist. Despite any given ruse,
One must practice discretion before sipping fruit juice.

---

49 Horton, pun on Horton hears a who. **Horton** the Elephant struggles to protect a microscopic
community from his neighbors who refuse to believe it exists. Book by Dr. Seuss.

STARBUCKS® DEMEANOR

Although their armrests aren't draped in rich indigo velour,
the coffee behemoth has a knack for minted holiday décor.
If there's one caveat that even competitors can concur:
Starbucks won't invest corporate dollars into **IKEA**® furniture.
Three partners, inspired by a coffee roasting entrepreneur,
maintained the shop for sixteen years before deciding to transfer
to then employee Howard Shultz of the once fledging enterprise,
which has long since expanded to an international franchise,
offering professional care to each and every java consumer
be it a slack-jeaned teenager or an exalted baby boomer.
Since no corporation has stood without earning dissent,

with the muse at the ready, allow me to present
some feedback from peeved servers and miffed clients,
hoping the solution won't defy rocket science.
An experienced server can determine who you are
by the beverage you order from the counter or the car.
Black coffee drinkers tend to be straight-laced and mediocre,
likely to out themselves as an unabashed chain smoker.
Frappuccino® sippers just outgrew **Dora the Explorer**®
determined to steer the barista into sheer horror.
Chais are for hipsters; soccer moms prefer lattés.
Green tea anything seems to be the Asian craze.
Unfortunately, all Starbucks baristas aren't entitled to praise
as more customers vent on YouTube and shun accolades.
One coffee enthusiast grew enraged as she sped home
over her negligent server who left a copious amount of foam
in her cup after she specifically insisted it be foamless
One disabled, wheelchair-bound client fell under duress
when she spilled scalding coffee all over her outfit.
Apart from the manager, no one else worried about it.
On Santa Teresa Boulevard, one fifty-something Neanderthal
deposited two bottles of juice mixed with rubbing alcohol.
San Jose law officials nabbed her, thanks to an eye witness.
Luckily, zeroing in on murder suspects is everyone's business.
Starbucks coffee mongers as a whole don't appear at all nervous.
Thus the reason the corporation is unrivaled in customer service.

STEM CELLS! WHAT GIVES?

Barack Obama lifted federal funding restrictions on stem cell research,
angering some conservative Republicans and the Catholic Church.
This repeal will enable scientists and researchers with earnest intent
to cure patients and, calm donors with hard work and monies spent.
Prior to the Obama administration, President Bush vetoed
any medical legislation that spurred rights to an embryonic code.
In other words, he refused to sign or acknowledge any treatise
that involved seeking stem cells from an unborn fetus.
The headstrong war president held his stance, refusing to belong
to moderate viewpoints he considered dead wrong.
Further condemning the study was Senator John McCain

as he maintained his platform during the presidential campaign.
What if the campaign supporters of the Vietnam veteran
fully understood the potential of regenerative medicine?
Therapy in which physicians and analysts didn't bemoan
cases stemming from a damaged nerve to a broken bone.
Opposition aims to discourage or at least postpone
the inevitable blueprint to the dreaded human clone.
With the populace charged on popcorn and sci-fi movies,
why else would society overlook a possible cure for diabetes?
Or solving the mystery leading to Parkinson's disease?
Few realize some of the controversial study's benefactors
became household names like western and fantasy actors.
Nancy Reagan fought tooth and nail for the Bush White House
to relax federal constraints in attempts to aid her spouse.
The Reeve foundation[50] commended Obama for his decision.
Even "Superman" foresaw the benefits without x-ray vision.
In support of the effort worldwide, countries such as Greece,
Denmark, Sweden, South Korea, and Holland loosely police
restrictive standards on their ground breaking research
while Austria, Germany, and Portugal foster the church.
Perhaps it's best to follow suit and watch progress with suspicion.
Perhaps it's best to regard critics with straitlaced intuition.
Perhaps it's easier to deal with patients who rely on prosthetics
than to compromise moral, religious or spiritual ethics.

50   The *Christopher & Dana Reeve Foundation* is a charitable organization headquartered in Short Hills, New Jersey and dedicated to finding treatments and cures.

STILL OFF THE HOOK

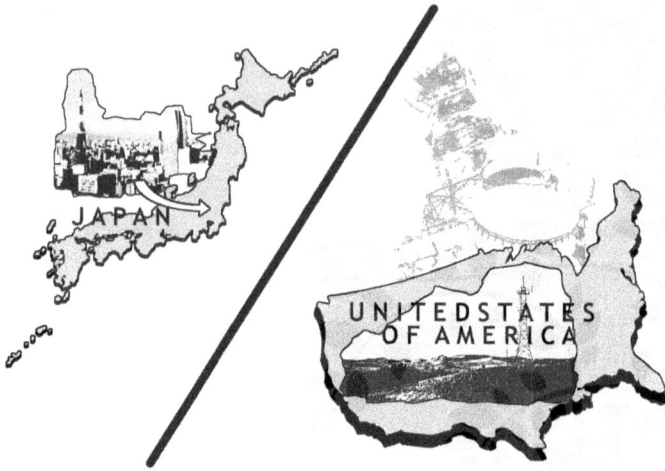

Color me old fashioned, but I have always hated
paying for electronic gadgets I felt were overrated.
For years, I enjoyed music on cassettes or vinyl,
now avoiding audio CDs is naught but sheer denial.
Some drivers stress the brilliance of owning a digital map
outweighs opening a **Rand McNally®'s** in your lap.
Granted, eyeballing a grid map while cruising the interstate
is gambling with life. Who couldn't relate?
But credit cards over cold cash? Who do you thank
when card scammers are racing you to the bank?
Well, I cringed a little over paying for a cell phone
preferring my laptop instead since I'm usually alone.
But I was always misplacing that damn **Motorola®.**

Why need I be on call? I am not the Ayatollah.
Yet one mishap convinced me to keep it in the glove
while driving when a consequential push came to shove:
After another night of commuting home from school
in my gas guzzling Caprice that made me a fool:
Driving while chatting with a long distance flame,
for privacy's sake, I needn't mention her name.
Choosing the online company of an effortless flirt
I failed to notice the illuminating engine oil alert.
Suddenly, a rumbling noise erupted from beneath the hood;
I veered to the right shoulder as well as I could.
Examining the damage, I surmised I needed a tow
Understandably, my **Chevy**® dealt me its final blow.
With no mobile handy, I was left out to dry
except one bizarre option I fancied to try:
I urged my girlfriend in Okinawa, Japan
to contact my family as quickly as she can.
Telling my folks I was stranded in her improvised English
subjected her to a mild state of anguish.
My contact was bound by a thirteen hour time difference.
She lost her appetite for breakfast, not for suspense.
My folks sent a tow truck driver on the way.
I had two Franklin notes --barely enough to pay.
All was A-Okay but that vehicle was history.
How little time was spent in itself was a mystery.
My better half ensured I learned my lesson well
verbally cannon-balling me straight to hell!
Insisting that having a online laptop was no excuse;
and if I attempted that again she'd cut me loose!

TAILS FROM THE AUTO REPAIR SHOP

Don't you wish you could catch grease monkeys red-handed
before you spin out of the driveway and take you for granted?
I swear the auto mechanic sequenced that baby boomer
all around oldie but goodie station on my FM tuner.
Imagine maniacal Presley fans at the bingo raves
requesting that "Hound Dog" anthem on the air waves.
While the deejay spins crusty 45s on a wobbly turntable,
nostalgia slapped me with an Aesop fable:
an old bloodhound, reveling in his days of youth, revealed
a stalwart devotion to the owner everyday in the field.
The cur redoubled his efforts to hunt groundhogs, rabbits,
mountain lions, or worse due to mere stubborn habits.
As time prevailed, he faltered, his strength diminished
yet his unflinching fidelity was far from finished.

One hunting afternoon, the hero accosted a wild boar,
clamped the beast's ear, and his decrepit jaw went sore,
decayed fangs deceived him, enabling the boar to flee.
The peeved witness swooped down, cracked a branch upon his knee,
flogged the aged servant incessantly until the hound cried,
"Master, I beg! Spare me at once, let the punishment slide:
blame my strength and my teeth, namely, no sense of fear
overwhelmed me when I seized that prize boar by the ear,
nor was I remotely timid, skeptical or nervous
This failure was met with immaculate service"
One must never allow past diligence to be forgotten.
Remember that the next time your car goes rotten.
While driving, please excuse my reckless bouts of escape
whenever I'm texting or listening to books on tape
from a college induced lecture to Intro to psychology
or a segmented version of a Norton Lit anthology.
And the speaker dictates, with a steady mentality,
that the pituitary gland controls one's personality.
I wish that speaker was Mikhail Bulgakov[51].
I'd pay double for his stand up at the Addison Improv.
The aforementioned penned the novella *A Dog's Heart.*
Apart from Communist Russia censuring his satirical art,
the tale revolves around a homeless cur whose new owner
implants the sexual organs of a malevolent donor.
What results is the evolution of a once domestic dog
to an ungrateful man hound prone to scathing dialogue,
and unspeakably deviant forms of loutish behavior
to the effect the surgeon granted the staff a disfavor.
One lesson as sharp as the razor piercing its gut:
Never take advantage of an unfortunate mutt!

---

51   Mikhail Bulgakov, best known for his novel *The Master and Margarita,* which has been called one of the
masterpieces of the 20th century.

TALES FROM THE BACKSIDE

My brother got a warning call from Time Warner Cable,

explaining that his data fiber connection may run unstable.

Instead of telling him whether new ramifications must be set,

they claimed Kardashian resolved to "break the Internet[52]."

At first, he laughed out loud, recognizing a prank call,

but then the Wi-Fi on my handheld began to stall.

Nostradamus predicted the era of the big booty apocalypse,

stating a woman of mixed heritage and fifty inch hips.

would soon overtake the celebrity world by storm,

her voluptuous derriere dictating the societal norm.

In the big booty apocalypse you should cast your votas.

Which female celebrity in Hollywood has the best nalgotas?

It only took one sex tape to garner mass appeal.

Even her detractors insist her butt is not real.

But scintillating socialites like Paris Hilton defied

---

52   "break the Internet." On the cover of Paper, her nude buttocks are featured above the caption: "Break the Internet"

the "diva-licious" trend while lacking a prominent backside.
As for unsung models, consider Buffie the Body
who modeled for top brands like Azzure Denim and, allegedly, Bacardi.
Video vixen Bria Myles, underground stunner. Nearly lost my mind
thinking she lost her mind, too, when she shrunk her behind.
Considering the cutthroat catcallers chasing "junk in the trunk,"
some girls were adversely affected, and so their ego shrunk.
If you thought the slip-on buttocks in the seventies were outrageous,
the interest in PMMA[53] butt injections got contagious.
For Apryl Michelle Brown, the cause of a black-market injection
stemmed from "pancake butt" jokes that she felt needed correction.
Those procedures led her to a near death staph infection.
She started a website sending women in the right direction,
conveying that women of all sorts are created beautiful,
from the top of their heads to their toenail cuticle.
Enter the bombshell from the Bronx named Jennifer Lopez
who performed as a Fly Girl from *In Living Color* with Rosie Perez.
Her talents as a singer and, an actress, combined with callipygian[54] traits,
helped her hold her own with the finest bubble butt heavyweights.
Miley Cyrus, that bidding Mouseketeer of "Wrecking Ball" acclaim,
brought back the sacred art of twerking into mainstream fame.
Although its popularity resurged, most were unimpressed
since the junk in Miley's trunk was a barren sight at best.
Maybe if a philanthropist at heart would have been the answer:
Who couldn't picture Christina Applegate twerking for cancer?
Sir Mix-a-lot celebrated the twentieth anniversary of "Baby Got Back".
Nicki Minaj fans helped promote "Anaconda," photoshopping her asscrack.
In the big booty apocalypse you should cast your votas.
Which female celebrity in Hollywood has the best nalgotas[55]?

---

53   polymethyl-methacrylate
54   Callipygian, high brow diction for big butt.
55   Nalgotas, the spanish word for big buttcheeks, not ass.

TEN HOURS WALKING AS A WOMAN IN NYC

I'm certain the whole world has heard the news
about the Shoshana Roberts's video that spawned forty million views
for walking for ten hours. Wasn't she exhausted?
Wasn't she harassed? Wasn't she accosted?
"Hollaback[56]" convinced the actress she was flattering eye candy
for the working class Cheech and Chong, Amos and Andy.

---

56   Hollaback, photoblog and grassroots initiative to raise awareness about and combat street harassment.

I'm certain that Tarantino appreciates the diction.
Review the Jack Rabbit Slim's scene in "Pulp Fiction".
Granted, even for New York City it's ruefully shocking
to garner one hundred catcalls based on where you're walking.
Young women shouldn't have to don poker faces
to simply saunter out and about on a day-to-day basis.
No detractor should openly do these creeps a favor
and attempt to condone their immature behavior.
Put yourself in their shoes. How would you escape
the odds of sexual assault, battery, or rape?
I knew of one charmer that would have done all he can
to address Shoshana with respect was Compliment Man.
Ronald Milton's allure was a mainstay in Adams Morgan
without reeking of stale cocktails, scotch, or bourbon.
He greeted all couples, or ladies sauntering alone.
Hailed cabs for stumblers, and escorted drunks home.
Washington, saddened by his plans to move to Florida,
should have sent the hero beaming in a Crown Victoria.
The local legend showered women with accolades for years.
In his passing, Jacksonville paid tribute, half in tears.
YouTube vloggers, half-starved for viral attention,
prepared a litany of parodies too unworthy to mention.
The staged videos that have littered the computer screen
involve walking as Princess Leia, a skateboarder, a drag queen,
a hipster, Batman, and other clowns strutting their privilege,
this woman collects death threats for conveying a message.
It's high time that men heed our wakeup call
and exercise finer methods for the PUA[57] protocol.

---

57   PUA, pick-up artist

THE ALMIGHTY PAT ROBERTSON

I wonder what con artist on earth can ruthlessly persist
to amass a cult following as a televised evangelist?
I'm apathetic to thrill seekers being duped in a sketchy environment.
I'm not amused when baby boomers lose two thirds of their retirement.
Whether it was destined to meet the hands of the Blackjack dealer,
or destined to "make it rain[58]" on topless strippers swilling "El Tesoro" tequila,
the prime members of the psychic community be funded to research
the dubious activities that continue within the range of the church.
Detractors insist people must accept the cards life dealt.
And all gullible saps are fair game in the Bible Belt.

---

58 "make it rain", When you have a wad of cash and throw it in the air in a strip club.

So let's discuss Pat Robertson and what made him famous.
what made him legendary, what made him shameless.
He received admission to Lexington's Washington and Lee
where he finished magma cum laude with a history degree.
With the First Marine Division, Robertson earned the privilege
to receive awards for his painstaking role in "Heartbreak Ridge"
(just above the landmark of North Korea's Thirty-eighth Parallel)
where artillery, hope and frostbite were served cold in hell.
Where he failed in law, with divinity he realized his fate,
and founded the Christian Broadcasting Network in 1978.
Eight years later Chancellor Robertson confirmed rumors as valid.
He was seeking the presidential nomination on the Republican ballot.
He surrendered his credentials and the ministry to his son.
Albeit he gained millions rallying, the incumbent vice president won.
In foreign trade transactions, he made the best of the financial opportunity.
Robertson had an infamous stance in the overseas business community:
Human rights activists deemed him oblivious to moral scrutiny:
vivified as an unscrupulous bandit who operates without impunity
In the midst of a Bank of Scotland deal tailored as a joint venture,
Robertson's criticism of homosexuals was met with due censure,
sabotaging the agreement. Rescue supply pilots flew to Zaire
to assist Rwandan refugees in dire need of welfare.
Instead of providing relief to genocide victims, they hauled a shipment
of stir pans, conveyors, and other tools of diamond dredging equipment.
Another business deal whisked away in dismal failure
was contracted with the slain Liberian president Charles Taylor.
In front of the international tribunal, Taylor testified
his ally Robertson volunteered to make his case when he relied
on the African president to make concessions for his mining operation,
allowing Liberians a 15 percent stake after the gold exploitation.
 I'm unmoved by his exploits, and I don't sponsor character defamation
provided he doesn't act in the hallowed name of salvation.

THE BLOCK IS HOT

L'il Wayne claimed recently he will embrace his final stint
as the flagstaff artist of the Young Money Records imprint.
I saw a video on You Tube® of him explaining his album delay.
He felt his product was unfinished, and it had to convey
a far more polished embodiment of his painstaking work;
some time after his announcement, he just went berserk.
If you're a fan of the Carter, you already know how come:
He asserted the label manager refused to release his album.
Maybe the executives felt urged to exert their privilege.
Maybe the executives concurred the music was garbage.

Maybe the executives' investors should have reconsidered
the tweeted messages to the fans now left embittered.
Despite artistic differences, Shrimp Daddy built the bridges
that connected the Universal label to the road of the riches.
I am fond of L'il Wayne but I respect Dwayne Michael Carter.
Plus I'm surprised the Birdman turned him into a martyr.
At first, I was disgusted with his tattooed appearance,
denouncing his parents for their lack of interference.
But then he produced a DIY video for his viewing audience,
and hoped the listeners based their actions with common sense.
He addressed his drank consumption, also known as Texas tea;
That sizzurp. That lean. That syrup. That purple jelly.
His physician prescribed medicines similar to medical marijuana
to rid him of demons that feed on his personal trauma.
And he queried his fan base on the reasons they chose
to mar their body with graffiti straight down to their toes.
Our favorite Martian detailed how he's far from haughty
after purchasing a skate ramp, guitars, and a spanking Bugatti.
What I gathered is that the man had a strong conviction
to act as such and wasn't susceptible to a hopeless addiction.
In other moments, the mainstream rapper joked and laughed
about pro athletes behind mixing boards, imitating his craft.
After his forty minute lecture, I finally understood;
how his strong work ethic propelled his livelihood,
how his decisions are seldom based on societal pressures;
how his children act in the house are delicate measures.

THE CASSETTE TAPE CULTURE

Apart from Generation X-ers, honestly, no one expects
any young blood to recall that famous slogan from Memorex®.
"Is it live or..." How about the Hitachi Maxell's® campaign?
Then let's rekindle our thoughts back to memory lane:
In steps a white gloved servant with a handlebar moustache
approaching a mysterious man in **Ray Ban**® panache.
"The usual?" He asks. The man replies in kind, "Please."
The butler cues a cassette from Wagner's "*Ride of the Valkyries.*"
Thirty mile an hour winds devour him in his armchair,
but it fails to dishevel his feathery, sandy blond hair.
That breakthrough ad was incredibly hard to forget
since it's an iconic stamp of the audio cassette.
Considering the time spent during my audio upbringing
I thank God my eardrums are no longer ringing.
My generation is well read in the arts of tape fundamentals:

We know how to rewind them with number two pencils.
We know how to sense when a tape-mangling boom box
will destroy the magnetic strip before the tape deck locks.
If you were an allowance deprived youngster, the only place to go
to record your favorite hits back then was the FM radio.
I used to record the master mixes from mainstream radio's Q107
with the el cheapo cassettes purchased from 7Eleven.
The weekend meant "Breaker's Delight" with DJ Frank Ski.
The tuning dial was already sequenced on the **JVC**®.
The tuning dial was already sequenced on stations with gritty AM static.
This all meant nothing to a thirsty cassette tape fanatic.
Back then, no one amassed more music than me…
except Grandma, and she attended a Protestant ministry.
Sometimes, your collection of mixtapes also depended
on your particular social circles and who you befriended.
Dubbing music from the radio was the thing in grade school
but, by eighth grade those "home tapes" were so uncool.
We embraced a new device that came into play:
The advent of the **VHS**® player came our way.
Even recording *Yo! MTV Raps* and the *Headbanger's Ball*
showed no signs or symptoms of cassette tape withdrawal.
From boom box to car stereo, they were indispensable.
To leave home without one was incomprehensible.
Although, cassette tapes were relished in adolescence,
I'd rather see them coveted as beloved obsolescence.
I'd rather see a nonunion executive at **TDK**® stifle
the revival of the cassette tape with a loaded assault rifle.
Here's some rhetoric you won't find at all strange:
How can you expect progress if you can't embrace change?
Go slowly, if you must, on your way to the attic,
and discard those clumps of plastic,
you tape hoarding fanatic.

THE CHICANO MOVEMENT

Want to know what online podcast infringes on my conservative limits?
The Loud Speakers Network presentation called *The Brilliant Idiots*.
Their team players the *Breakfast Club* radio host Charlemagne tha God
and *Wild 'n Out* comedian Andrew Schulz create the two-man squad.
Together they discuss pop culture with such an unapologetic stance,
they keep bodyguards on the payroll to knock brawlers in a trance.
Their wit remained incisive as a knife with a serrated edge
when interviewing hip hop radio personality, Rikki Martinez.
Not to be confused with the likes of singer, Ricky Martin,
the Menudo one hit wonder who sold records by the carton.
Rikki is spelled with two "K's" as in "Kim Kardashian,"
King Kong®, Krispy Kreme's®, and, at least, for the time being,

meaning Martinez is the California native's maiden name;
so interested suitors need to prepare their "A" game.
While chatting about her moral upbringing and Chicano roots,
the KPWR radio host alluded to the craze of zoot suits.
A chapter in the culture stemming from the *Zoot Suits Riots*
where local residents against naval servicemen staged defiance.
When I hear of zoot suits, I think about Cab Calloway
and the Harlem Renaissance embodied in Billie Holiday.
Despite sauntering in the Gas Lamp District's strip plaza,
I faintly recall any distinct cultural relics from La Raza.
I'm aware of the Black Panther response to the Watt's melees
even heard of the Asian Tigers, but not the Brown Berets.
One common misconception found among most outsiders
felt African Americans started the culture of low riders.
I left clicked on the mouse to place the radio show on pause,
and googled the names of contributors to the Chicano cause.
First thing I learned about was the Great Wall of Los Angeles;
to come to California and overlook this mural is scandalous!
Judith F. Baca's mission employed over four hundred people
to emboss historical accounts of the Golden State's social upheaval.
Cesar Chavez co-founded the National Farm Workers Association
along with Delores Huerta to spearhead the foundation.
The HBO film based on the Vietnam era's barrage of heated bouts
protesting the California education system: *The Chicano Blowouts*,
irate over the sky high wartime minority casualty rate
and other token of injustices incurred on March 6, 1968.
The Internet's a boon for finding ethnic snapshots,
should you choose to zoom in and connect the cultural dots.

THE CRIME WIZARDS OF OZ

I never seem to overcome that midday shock,
that hysterical blaring coming from my alarm clock.
I prepped the water heater for my Hollywood shower,
judging whether lemons go best with a Whisky Sour.
Hmmm. Granny Smith apples dipped in *soju*[59]
taste yummier than last night's excuse for tofu.
Then my eyes glazed with surprise over the Internet;
a miracle arose from the said medical threat.
Fate gave a lost girl a second chance:
this teen, still awestruck by her circumstance,
waited four months for an organ advance,

---

59 Soju, a distilled beverage containing ethanol and water.

after enduring two failed heart transplants.
Wait a second. One. But imagine the sacrifices
met relying on artificial heart devices!
Exasperated to revel and share the good news,
I emailed the Tin Man—who else would you choose?
The Tin Man ran a lumber firm in Southeast Alaska
until timber shares fell, triggering a downhill fiasca:
His wife Rosie[60] left him plus he never discusses
the Mafia smelting his mother to build steel trusses.
I queried on how Governor Palin's doing.
"Fantastic," he replied, stating she's pursuing
a natural gas pipeline plan that minimizes offsets
by Greenpeace yet maximizes state profits.
But Murkowski[61] insists her strategy will fail
unless resounding disputes with **Exxon Mobil**® prevail.
But before passing judgment on Palin's Alaska,
consider the juvenile issues in Heinemann's Nebraska.
Remember Dorothy, that freckled face wanderer?
She networks with the Wizard, an underground child launderer,
She's a no-nonsense trafficker taking various bids,
passing as a **Wal-Mart**® trucker kidnapping kids,
tossing them in Omaha thanks to "safe haven" laws,
holding no regrets to her baseless cause.
Tales of her exploits drew a definite pause;
that stiletto heel clicker that fled from Oz
thrives on the innocent to fuel her career,
yet revised legislation is coming forth this year.
I sighed in relief, rest assured that hope
will continue to victor if we continue to cope.

---

60   Rosie, the household robot from an American animated sitcom *The Jetsons* produced by Hanna-Barbera,
61   Frank Murkowski was a United States Senator from Alaska from 1981 until 2002.

THE FOOD BABE

Why is it when a faceless entity launches a fierce campaign,
the public feels empowered to tackle Adversity's terrain
but when a bold underdog wants to fight for the cause,
the vultures of dissent tear them apart with incisive claws?
Remember that meme comparing the Monsanto chicken
to the chemical free chicken that made your blood thicken?
One champion for food justice emerged from the flanks,
and demanded answers when the bigwigs drew blanks.
One noted blogger, author, and indefatigable activist
confronts food industry policies with a vegan fist,
addressing health concerns with majors like Chipotle®,

Kraft®, Chick-fil-A®, Panera®—even Jared's Subway[62]®.
Vani Hari regretted her eating habits while at the hospital
undergoing an appendectomy. No longer was it possible
to sustain with the old routine of chemically treated food;
that's how the Food Babe developed a new attitude.
She waged war against Subway, garnering 50,000 signatures,
to remove flour bleaching agents and dough conditioners
from their breads. Later NPR[63] performed their due diligence
and the experts denied any health risks in the bleaching agents,
despite the banning of azodicarbonamide overseas.
Kraft foods was the next corporation to buckle to her pleas.
The Food Babe pushed for dye removal in their Mac & Cheese.
348,000 votes moved the corporation's Board of Trustees.
To beverage conglomerates, Hari continued to push
famed breweries like Miller Coors® and Anheuser Busch®
to print their trade ingredients with her blogging theatrics.
Her detractors noted how Hari relishes in fear mongering tactics.
Scientists state the computer science grad makes pejorative claims
On any given chemicals featured with odd sounding names.
The medical community worldwide reserved their patience
when the Food Babe questioned the effectiveness of vaccinations.
Another example of Hari's shortfalls is her reliance
to cite Dr. Masuru Emoto, a believer of pseudoscience,
insisting undesirable feelings can pollute drinking water;
at this point, readers start to wonder who is the real martyr.
It's understandable to harbor opinions in the beginning
of research but it's the evidence that keeps the populace winning.
Or else the real food experts will lampoon hack journalism,
and banish the freedom fighters back into their blogging prism.

---

62   Jared Fogle, once spokesman for Subway restaurants.
63   **National Public Radio (NPR)** is a privately and publicly funded non-profit membership media
      organization.

THE HOLIDAY SCAMMERS

During the yuletide season, no one at all finds it odd
that scammers come in flocks to commit gift card fraud.
Although holiday gift certificates are no longer the norm,
the entire gift card industry definitely needs a reform.
In the late nineties, gift cards bumrushed the retail scene
until the sensation of plastic became shopaholic routine.
Sneaky fees went unnoticed until consumers grew cautious.
Fight Back! episodes with Dave Horowitz made me nauseous.
The fine print allowed merchants to sponge off a monthly surcharge
while it lies in the scrap drawers of your parents' garage.

Whose fault was it to pay no attention to the "dormancy fees[64]"?
Whose fault was it to disregard major big business policies?
The underwriters, my friend—don't you credit yourself.
Store retailers insure you won't pocket the wealth.
Negligent customers are susceptible to "breakage,"
in which snatching funds from the card is a privilege.
Even state governments sharpen their talons and claws
due to broad stipulations in their municipal laws.
As a faithful friend and consumer you should consume
an **Outback**® steak by Easter and not wait until June.
The onus is yours! Don't tarnish your precious reward card.
Besides, there's another reason to be on your guard.
For instance, buying reward cards right off the display rack
can be accessible to thieving staff members to hack.
Buying a gift card with a stolen **Visa**® **or American Express**®
is the number one contender for gift giver stress.
It doesn't matter whether you find your transaction amiss,
hold on dearly to your receipt as noted proof of purchase.
Doling out personal information is a definite no-no.
Setting restrictions to store outlets is the best way to go.
So if you aren't mindful of handling the dollar almighty,
leave it up to the strip mall to keep your balance book tidy.

---

64   Dormancy fees had been imposed by some banks on credit card accounts that go dormant or unused
      for a certain period of time.

THE ICARUS CLAUS

Thumbing through an anthology of Grecian folklore
smothered in cobwebs at a bargain bookstore,
I came across the tale of the folly of the Sun
as told by the poet Ovid or, rather, his rendition.
The Sun's palace stood high on pillars of gold.
Intricate paintings abound with mysteries untold.
In stepped an interloper in the form of a youth
accompanied by his grievance to discover the truth.
His lips parted, then froze, as if he feared to bother

asking, "My mother insisted that you are my father.
The boys tease me and taunt me everyday at my school,
chiding my mates for befriending a fool!"
Helios responded, "Yes, Phaethon, I am he,
and to further convince you, I shall agree
to grant you anything as my solemn oath,
this proposal need only be recognized by us both!"
With gleaming eyes, "Since you're zealous to abide
by your word, I wish to experience one chariot ride."
Holding that thought and page with a bookmarked finger,
the hypothetical premise began to linger:
What kind of drama would have occurred
if his father were Santa Claus, and he kept his word?
Phaethon would have treaded snow fallen savanna
and the icy terrain of Bozeman, Montana!
Father and son together with those androgynous elves
dusting off the loaded rifles hung on the shelves,
chasing Dasher, Donner, and Rudolph for one reason
to scalp their furry heads for antler hunting season.
I reopened the paperback and continued reading.
Helios, with raised eyebrows, fell aghast. "My heart is bleeding!
Son, you're inexperienced. Even a seasoned chariot driver
couldn't handle a day's journey as a mortal survivor.
My unbridled horses will sense the slack in their reins.
The savage beasts of the zodiac will attack like hurricanes!
Please look around. Phaeton, I offer my entire
palace of light if you wish! Please refrain from this one desire."
The pleas of Helios yet fell on deaf ears,
rash mind and stubborn heart, which heightened his fears.
Dawn was approaching. Stars vanished. Horses waited.
Phaethon would embark on his adventure anticipated.
The East Winds offered very little turbulence,

but the steeds gradually sensed a human presence.
Escalating to the high heavens, he felt the essence
of a Sky Titan exuding from his adolescence.
Suddenly, the great chariot rattled in an awkward motion,
and the driver had forsaken his triumphant devotion.
He lost the reins. And the horses left the beaten trail
and ran amuck, and the charioteer's pulse was frail.
He narrowedly missed the great Scorpion's sting,
and one of the fiery horses singed the Lion King.
And again the chariot climbed higher and higher
in the sky, then plummeted, setting the world on fire.
Mountain springs evaporated. Forests left in smoldering ashes.
Nature repressed her tears under lush eyelashes.
Mother Earth pleaded to the heavens and recommended
that the terror reigned upon her be abruptly ended.
At once, Jove seized one of his piercing thunderbolts
and delivered a fatal blow to the driver and the colts.
Poor Phaethon spiraled down from the purple skies
into the river Eridanus[65], unseen by mortal eyes.
The naiads felt pity for the teenager's doom,
buried him, and engraved upon his tomb:

> Here lies the remains of an unsung daredevil
> who defied his limits to reach his father's level

Should youthful exuberance yield to seasoned experience
and remain sheltered, assured, and without repentance?

---

65   river Eridanus, a river in Greek mythology, somewhere in Central Europe, which was territory that
      Ancient Greeks knew only vaguely

THE WONDERFUL WORLD OF DORITOS®

What other snack can better complement guacamole or cheese dips
after you've depleted your family-sized serving of Doritos corn chips?
For starters, there are grilled cheese sandwiches, baked potatoes,
buffalo wings, and taco salads garnished with diced tomatoes.
My conservative palate yields for toasted triangles, carrots or celery sticks.
My face palm response discourages new-wave culinary tricks.
The chip inventor, Arch West, who left the earth at aged ninety-seven
is enjoying a tortilla smorgasbord at a snack convention in heaven.
"Nacho average burial service," the online enquirer TMZ did learn
the family plans to sprinkle tortilla shells over his urn.
"Doritos," derived from Mexican Spanish, means "turned golden or crisp."
"Crisp" is English vernacular for "chips" pronounced with a lisp.

My youthful craving for bagged treats started with **Cheetos**®
but that cheesy residue was finger licking filthy, so I switched to **Fritos**®.
But "when I became a man, I gave up my childish ways"
Corinthians 13:11 left me spiraling towards my Doritos craze.
Frito-Lay launched a contest with one million dollars as the drawing prize.
For Chris Capel this event became a subtle blessing in disguise.
His five offerings were selected from the sea of four thousand submissions.
But I can't determine whether he's responsible for the angler renditions.
One of three fishermen sticks his Dorito-stained fingers into the water
only to catch a mermaid attached old enough to be his daughter!
Another commercial had me riling was entitled "Finger Cleaner"
Whether you find it gut-crunching hilarious depends on your demeanor.
Need I tell you there are even some commercials now banned from TV;
starring steamy sun-kissed savannahs sprinkling snacks over their bikinis.
Import the mainstay Canadian varieties for your next get-together;
imagine hors d'oeuvres laced with "Intense Pickle", "Zesty Cheese", "Jalapeño Cheddar,".
"Roulette" boasts piping hot flavors bound to leave you in a corner, slumped.
But the Japanese brands will see to it that you get your stomach pumped.
Would you dare offer the following goodies to next-door neighbors,
like their "Butter and Soy Sauce", "Salami" or "Wasabi" flavors?
Would the mutated cockroaches from the Fukushima lab
ingest products like "Corn Soup", "Stir Fry", "Winter Crab,"
"Garlic and Anchovy", "Coconut Curry", "Classic Salt with Grape Soda".
Even Monsanto cows will stare you down in South Dakota.
This is the country that manufactures soybean **Kit Kats**®.
Not all cases of halitosis can be resolved with wintergreen **Tic-tacs**®.
Granted, any committed tortilla lover should snack in moderation,
so don't go overboard when you see them waiting at the gas station.

THESE COLORS DON'T RUN

Given that only 15 percent of Americans own a US passport,
face it: International travel is a backpacker's resort.
Imagine all the seething, pent-up, maniacal frustration
if Phil Keoghan[66] begged John Doe to complete an application.
The Amazing Race rocked viewers, nailing fourteen seasons,
but main street is scared shitless for a thousand reasons.

---

66   host of the Amazing Race, reality television game show in which contestants travel worldwide.

They don't speak English! No freedom of expression!
They want to teach us young infidels a lesson.
It's an option only the upscale wealthy can afford,
that cold cash could have financed a late model Accord.
Who's going to muster all the planning, the anticipation
when corporate America offers a two-week vacation?

Why bother going abroad? We have the Florida Everglades.
Disneyworld® South by Southwest. The **Macy**® Parades.
Appalachian Mountains. Niagara Falls. Yosemite Park.
The Grand Canyon. The Smithsonian. Broadway after Dark.
Why should we concern ourselves with foreign cultures
when New York's flooded with immigrating vultures?

Media outlets contribute to our narcissistic position,
from gripping current events to intriguing murder fiction:
Jack the Ripper forewarned flappers of the London fog;
Tarantino[67] convinced moviegoers of sadists in Prague.
Terrorists bombed nightclubs in cosmopolitan Bali.
Captain Hook's no threat for the swashbuckling Somali.
Add Dubya berating world players as the Axis of Evil.
How can fellow Americans see past the social upheaval?
With an apathetic Washington rewording foreign policy,
is weak regard for the world our contributing fallacy?

But this American generation welcomes Japanese imports.
Falafel stands. Sudoku. Muay Thai kickboxing sports.
No shame in exploring the land of our Founding Fathers.
So turn a deaf ear to liberals and whoever it bothers.

---

67   American movie director that introduced the horror flick Hostel to moviegoers in 2006.

ZONE OUT

"My name is Talky Tina, and I'm going to kill you."
The master of suspense had a thousand ways to fill you
with anxiety, horror, pensive moments of intrigue,
captivating new listeners in the sci-fi league.
Why isn't the "Twilight Zone" series held in acclaim
as "Star Trek" or "Star Wars" where it birthed its fame?
Trekkie conventions pay top dollar to see William Shatner,
but the "Twilight Zone" gave rise to that acting disaster!

"Star Wars" die-harders parodied the franchise with "Fanboys",
and the Rotten Tomatoes review gave it considerable noise.
Didn't the effects of the Syracuse native's sci-fi stinger
leave the audience tenser than Han Solo's trigger finger?
Didn't the effects of turning **Chatty Cathy**® into a vengeful doll
make loners swear off silicon **Barbies**® and alcohol?
Serling balanced concepts fraught with spills and chills
to mirror society's image and address social ills.
Let's take a moment to celebrate the iconic show
that grandfathered the culture and subgenres to follow.
Remember the episode that had humanity shook,
pledging "to serve man"? The perfect cookbook.
That's episode eighty-nine from the "Twilight Zone" anthology.
Another show that pecks at the depths of psychology
was the show with a girl trapped in another dimension;
that had hard-nosed heart strings standing at attention.
The movie "Poltergeist" was inspired by "Little Girl Lost",
in which Father rushed in to rescue Bettina at any cost.
And there were subtle themes like "the Bewitchin' Pool"
where Sport and Jeb were subjected to cruelty and ridicule.
The two children into the swimming pool descended deeper
to rekindle compassion met with a "motherly" Grim Reaper.
Score credits for the episodes belong to Bernard Herrmann,
Jerry Goldsmith, and others who carried the melodic burden.
Just an afterthought of Goldsmith's work, before memory escapes:
he composed the score for "Basic Instinct" and "Planet of the Apes".
And as Herrmann, a great deal of his motion picture stock
rides on his collaborative efforts with Alfred Hitchcock.
Hilarious comedy spinoffs pay homage to the syndication.
For instance, the Simpsons' rendition of the "Poltergeist" situation.
Serling's marvels in Hollywood would have gone unrefined
without his activist outlook urging each viewer to free his mind.

Spoilers

SPOILERS

～๑ A Dose of Determination ๑～

I recently headed to Walgreen's to purchase an 32 ounce bottle of Listerine and a pair of flip flops. I started up the car, cued up my radio station and arrived before I knew it. I thought to myself how toll roads are seldom under construction and marveled that the "free" roads usually need maintenance. Before I reach the double doors, I saw a hawk swoop down and attack a pigeon with vigor. I aggressively scared away the hawk from the pigeon by honking my car horn. While waiting in the checkout line, I decided to peel open a tabloid. I read about two stories, one featuring a person with tattoos covering every inch of her body, the other a surfing zealot that was accosted by a shark. Both stories expand on a fit of determination. Upon leaving the store, I realized the hawk was also a determined soul. The feathered hunter left behind a ravaged flock of several headless pigeons in the parking lot.

～๑ A Very Rapey Christmas Carol ๑～

This entry discusses the history, adaptations and varying perspective s of the 1940's song, "It's Cold, Outside."

～๑ Airline Antics ๑～

The work opens up introducing the reader to many annoying types of passengers that board aircrafts. One account involves an executive, quizzing a worker about nuts. The other struggles with the headache of bringing an emotional support pet on board a plane. Of course, these are the rare and extreme instances of flight drama. Frequent flyers experience many troublesome passenger antics on various flights. This piece also offers methods of dealing with the problem.

⌐◉ As The World Turns, The Flu Returns ◉⌐

The first sixteen lines discuss the hardships concerning the swine flu in Mexico. According to weather and news reports, there have been fantastic changes due to the fear of swine flu. Some positive changes that have incurred include Cleaner air, and lessened noise pollution. Egyptian military and farmers cooperated for the sake of preserving their livestock. Although China was occupied with its measures on avian flu, the government treated Mexicans in their country harshly. Despite the clash among international politicians, international scientists are cooperating to stop the viruses.

⌐◉ Bowl for Peace Before Your Pins Get Struck Down ◉⌐

The poem starts with the response of the listener after being told of an alleged account from a paranoid bowler. Instead of receiving sympathy, the speaker reminds him or her of why they bowl. It is used as a form of meditation to "escape" the misery of the news reports.

⌐◉ But Is It Just? ◉⌐

This poem involved a strange criminal court case with a disabled man. While physically unable to hold his hand up, he was found in possession of a handgun. You might infer that the possible injustice occurred due to Mercer County's need of cash. A clause in the possession laws holds him just as culpable as anyone else.

⁓☯ Care to Fly Malaysian Air? ☯⁓

This entry talks about various theories stemming from the mysterious disappearance of Flight 370. The theories of an invisible cloak wrapping the craft, North Korea seizing the craft, and various other situations cropped up.

⁓☯ Character Assassinated ☯⁓

Lance Armstrong is an amazing man. The moment he resolved to win his bout over cancer, he promised himself to become a champion for his cause. He fought to make a better life for cancer survivors. Although he bested his competitors through illegal methods, he was not alone in his steroid use. The sports federation was suspicious over the consequent wins during a seven-year period. As big box sponsors abandoned him and his own starter fundraiser ousted him, he never dismissed the patients that held onto his legacy to envision themselves as "cancer survivors."

⁓☯ Come Here My Love, Wait...Is That an Adam's Apple? ☯⁓

I like fast food, so I headed over to said restaurant. Unfortunately, I ordered something that didn't agree with me. I felt the need to take an antacid. Next, I asked where to get some breath mints. Lastly, I discussed how my night went last night. It was an event targeted for sexually adventurous individuals, unbeknownst to me. See what follows.

⁓☯ Compliment Battle Rap ☯⁓

By now, everyone has a rough impression of what battle rap is, due to the popularity of the movie 8 Mile. However, few ever thought the concept of friendly battle even existed. I cited examples using matches from Pat Stay vs. Rone and Greely vs. Barry.

⤙⤚ Curse Of the Hollywood Pharaoh ⤙⤚

The placement of the King Tut exhibit is explained here. Then I brought up the mysterious curse of King Tut's tomb. Later, I transition to the curse of Billy Bob Thornton, mentioning other actors that suffered tragedies while working with the actor. Later the topic shifts to birth and abortion issues.

⤙⤚ Don't Clown With Ronald ⤙⤚

Basically, the piece brings up the everyday health threat of McDonalds restaurants, but mentions that the restaurant also contributed to helping children all over the world. However, whenever people attempt to decry McDonalds, they tend to overlook their mission of personal responsibility.

⤙⤚ Don't Shoot ⤙⤚

This is an abstract of what incidents followed after the fatal shooting of Mike Brown, of Ferguson, Missouri. The incident allegedly was televised worldwide, and the world responded to the situation before the courts ever presided over the case.

⤙⤚ Don't Tease Me, Tijuana ⤙⤚

Finding myself bored around suppertime in San Diego, I take to the idea of heading to Tijuana, Baha California. Later I describe the scenes I encountered on Revolution Avenue. I see men waging bets for Jai Alai. While downing some cocktails, I gather that some beautiful woman is luring me to dance. I'm dancing with her on a crowded dance floor. But I sense someone else moving in, trying to pick my pockets. I break away, realizing that they are working together. Later, I order a meal at a popular restaurant chain. To pass the time, I found myself playing Genja with some kid at the restaurant. To my surprise, he revealed a bag of marijuana to me. A nearby policeman warned him with a finger motion. Eventually, overwhelmed by my quick escapade, I return to San Diego, feeling fortunate that I don't have to live that way.

Driving Culture in the USA

This article details the various courses the driving culture is headed. A whirling tailspin that involves high speed train transportation, falling gas prices, the Fast and Furious achievers, rider sharing apps, and green technology.

Evil Empire

Push activists to analyze and scrutinize everything. I mention incidents in which Bayer and Chiquita coercive practices became documented.

Faith Tested, Love Approved

There enters a group of divorced friends. They gather at the poker table talking about their lifestyles. Everyone is participating, except me. After a grueling run of trivia questions, they ask me how my relationship has been so successful over the years. I politely excuse myself from the scene. Even though the lady in my life knew how to thrill me, due to past dismal relationships, I always suspected her of being unfaithful. Being a sailor, I took an assignment that led me to the Netherlands. Upon reaching Amsterdam, after finishing work, me and some crewmembers head into the city. Upon enjoying the nightlife, it dawned on me how my belle was a true partner in my life. To the extent I feel remorseful for second guessing her. Toward the end of the tale, I call off the detective hired to spy on her.

God Save the Wolf

The Wolf explained his situation to the reader of why he landed himself back in prison. He suggested that he served ten years for racketeering for his mentor, a lamb, in organized crime. After serving his time, he reunited with his boss over the greens at the golf resort. When opportunity struck, he managed to kill and eat his former boss. Doing this left a bone lodged in his throat, giving him immense pain. When he offered a reward to pull out the bone, a stork on pension decided to help. After the bone was retrieved, the wolf reneged on his offer. As the story continued, he met a young woman waiting at the bus stop, and attempted to woo her. After receiving information on her whereabouts, he decided to catch up with her later that day. He catches up with Little Red Riding Hood, and figured he was in for a night of corruption. All of this, only to discover that she was married. She later accused the wolf of attempted rape. The story ended with a didactic slogan.

Going Back to Thailand

About eighteen lines into the work, I describe the sights and sounds of other passengers awaiting a flight to Bangkok. Upon hearing the overhead speaker blare that the aircraft is ready to get passengers, I daydream of the allures abound in Thailand. Towards the end of the poem, someone asks whether I'm still boarding, as I'm probably the last passenger left.

Heartache in Hindustan

"Fitting the description" phenomenon privy only to America. Police officers worldwide are pressured to "uncover" law breakers with suspect agendas. Enough law abiding citizens fall victim. In this tale, unsuspecting individuals in India are believed to be SIMI devotees, and persecuted as such. Naved and Afzal were at the right place at the wrong time.

Hot Dog. Hot Dog. Hot Diggity Dog!!

I talk about how rude it once was to turn down a plate as a guest. Also how, as a child, no one wanted to eat vegetables. Now, being a parent, how should I persuade my child to eat their food? So, I tell the child if he wants to become rich one day, he needs to learn how to eat like a champion, like Mr. Kobayashi. Then I read off the antics of the hot dog eating champ. I absolve myself of guilt by insisting I will do whatever it takes to see that my kid is well fed.

It's About to Go Down

Before you ask what a recent breakup has to do with a impromptu ride to the massage parlor, ask yourself why is it wrong to not attend one while having a girlfriend? Anyhow, the story starts with the hero checking the massage parlor in town. Right up to the time the massage begins, I read two articles. The anecdote features a prize-winning dog that traveled all over the country. The other tale centers on the Madoff scandal. Upon discussing the latter, I thanked the masseuse for the massage and left.

Japanese Horror

I start off ranting of how movie library culture has dissolved, thanks to the advent of automated kiosks. If you've ever spent time in Western Europe, you know this concept was long overdue in the States. But I don't want to be boxed in as a gung-ho moviegoer. I, then, proceed to criticize the Asian horror craze; only the psychological horror franchises that invaded the US box office.

Journalist's Code of Ethics

I hold that online journalists or bloggers aren't being held to any visible standards. There are no particular examples noted. I rely on all preachy peachy stuff.

⌐◦⌐ Love is Deaf, Dumb and Blind ⌐◦⌐

This focuses on the teenage years. After a day of classes, I was eager to head home and unload, racing to catch the public bus. Upon reaching the bus, one offloading passenger smiled at me at me as he got off. Confused, I got on. I was already standing on the first step and couldn't move further. A mentally-challenged woman decided to snag my arm and pet it as the bus sped. Remember, I already can't move. Somewhere on the bus, someone was laughing at me the whole time. The bus driver stopped at each station, hinting whether or not I wanted to get off. After a few stops, I relented and get off. As the next passenger boarded, I smiled at him in kind.

⌐◦⌐ Mass Hysteria, Just In Time for the Holidays ⌐◦⌐

I present to you a night of a twisted drunkard, and a day of a cranky coffee drinker. I slyly inject a play on words from a famous 1980's hip hop song. If you lisp the lines aloud, you may catch on. Afterwards, I read online two tragedies happening roughly in the same period: the attacks in Mumbai and the Black Friday events. The former killed about 200 people, the latter exchange, a Walmart greeter. Both stories are sad and pointless, depending on the reader's level of sympathy.

⌐◦⌐ Moon River ⌐◦⌐

This may be a tricky one to follow without reading the notes first. It is planned as a juxtapose of Breakfast at Tiffany's and the original 9/11. In the voice of Holly Golightly, from the novel's storyline,(not the movie), Holly recounts her tale of running to South America after being accused of acting as a drug mule, unbeknownst to her. She meets with the president of Chile Salvador Allende. She accompanies him everywhere, up to the point of the attack of his residence. Basically General Pinochet staged a successful coup d'etat, and Allende dies in office after giving his final address to the people.

Holly escapes unscathed, but returns to New York under a new identity.

✑ Mr. Chi-city ✑

One YouTube vlogger shares an intimate moment with his subscribers. He takes time out of his schedule to spend time with his longtime friend. There's nothing special about this, except he takes us along to the cemetery on a snowy day. He converses with him as if the tombstone responds to him. Overall, he stresses that he wants gun violence to end in Chicago. His most popular submission is the episode where he prepares his refrigerator with drinks targeted to his female acquaintance's needs. In another episode, he shows us how he fights a parking citation in court.

✑ Never Forget 9/12 ✑

This account describes the attack of the Twin Towers as an American on American territory, but outside of the contiguous forty-eight states. Although this tragedy was heartfelt worldwide, the reaction differed in intensity, or could have, in Guam.

✑ Panhandling Scammers ✑

I'm having a special dream that includes Latoya Jackson. She's giving me a back massage with Tiger Balm. All of a sudden, I get up from bed sweating, later preparing my tourist plan of the day. I get annoyed seeing clean shaven hustlers that get up earlier than I do to sit all day panhandling for food. Again, this is another rant session about suspect charities.

✑ Pole Position ✑

The first six lines depict imaginary renditions of hell in the mind of a tortured individual. Remaining in a semi-conscience situation, the dreamer is held against his will by a vindictive spouse and has yet to awaken from his slumber. Upon awakening late one "morning", he proceeds to harass his wife by howling rudely about sirloins, potatoes, and espresso. He's reluctant to allow his wife to take pole fitness classes without putting up a fight. He questions himself on why his emotions are overwhelming concerning the ordeal. Finally, in his mind, he succumbs and attempts to see the bigger picture.

Public Bus Hassles

I take you through a lifestyle of a typical bus passenger from childhood to adulthood. I offer situations for both cases. The public bus scenario widely televised on YouTube is the AC Transit Bus Fight. It is not the worst, but one of the most popular events that happen on the bus.

Rebating You in a Circle Jerk

Have you noticed how the big box stores stopped offering rebates to sell the merchandise? I have noticed the absence of these offers. However, years ago, I was a serious rebate seeking opportunist. At times, these dealers renege on their offers. this is a situation where the buyer should beware.

Retirement Issues

The reader is type cast as motivational speaker for prospective retirees. Upon congratulating the reader for their presentation at the seminar, the mentor recounts what points must be covered regarding increasing one's portfolio.

Sino-Aussie Relations on Rudd's Watch

Here I have an account that discusses Australian Prime Minister Kevin Rudd's relationship with the government of China. The trade pact involves mining exploits. Nothing detrimental to diplomatic interests, but there were plenty of embarrassing events that proceeded to bring both governments on edge.

Sleeping with the Enemy

I open the poem discussing choice events in the Holy Bible. I'm particularly interested in the backstabbing that happens between lovers. I touch upon two examples: Mel Gibson, actor in the Lethal Weapon franchise and Donald Sterling, former owner of L.A. Clippers.

Sneaker Wonderland

Houston has an annual sneaker convention. I'm the last person to take sneakers seriously but I acknowledge how important they are to some people. I name drop on popular brands in the 1980s, explain the difference between a sneaker head and a sneaker fiend. I bring up when the sneaker love culture started. Of course, I return back to Houston Sneaker Convention.

SNL Korea®

Lately, Saturday Night Live lost its mojo in my eyes. I recall the greats in the eighties worth staying up late watching. Admittedly, few skits have been memorable. Overseas, the concept of SNL hasn't taken hold well either. Other countries have refused to respond with interest. It has, however, done well in South Korea. I love the skits over there, but, at times, they seem insensitive to the viewers' feelings.

Something about a Glass of Orange Juice

With allegedly factual information online, I discuss the method by which orange juice stays fresh and tasty for months on end. Apparently, not only is orange juice as fresh as we would expect, I assume this information would take orange juice off of the commodities market.

❧ Starbucks Demeanor ☙

I wax poetic about the splendors of Starbucks. I touch briefly on the coffee chain's history. Also, taken from a barista's YouTube account, I describe what kinds of people order certain gourmet coffee drinks. I also mention a few wild incidents that happened at Starbucks.

❧ Stem Cells! What Gives? ☙

The Obama administration lifted bans on stem research. The writing entails the vetoing of stem cell legislation in the Bush White House, to the dismay of former first lady Nancy Reagan. Science fiction type exploits scare the populace. On the other hand, the Christopher Reeve foundation thanked Obama. Also, the Catholic Church is against research. Some nations move forward with continued research whereas other countries side with the church and protest such work.

❧ Still Off the Hook ☙

This narrative responds to having mixed feelings about personal consumption of technology. I never wanted to tote a cell phone. However, I loved having wifi and a laptop while traveling, even in the pre-tablet days. While on the highway, I was conversing with an overseas long distance girlfriend. Suddenly, the engine gave out on me, and my girlfriend asked where I placed my cell. I told her I didn't have one and pleaded with her to call my parents. I needed a ride and have the car towed. After that happened, I relented and bought my first phone.

❧ Tails From the Auto Repair Shop ☙

The poem starts off with a rank from the ordeal coming from the automotive repair shop. An allusion takes me nostalgically to an Aesop fable about an old dog loyal to its master. Then I bring up another story from the novella, a Dog's Tail. This novella is a very humorous tale of a human's brain being placed into a house pet. The madness unfolds when the reader learns that the brain was of a former convict.

Tales from the Backside

A sarcastic opener insists that the Kim Kardashian actually "broke the internet". Then, a tirade ensues about video vixens and Hollywood socialites. Furthermore, the health problems that hurt one client in pursuit of butt injections inspired an organization to bolster self esteem. The resurgence of twerking spearheaded by Miley Cyrus and Nicki Minaj antics is also reviewed in this piece. The anniversary of the song "Baby Got Back." may have landed at a time where some are reliving the desire for large behinds. Apparently there is still a population of individuals that still prefer this option.

Ten Hours Walking as a Woman in NYC

This is my perspective on the titled ordeal. They chose a woman that may garner many cat calls from mostly black and Latino men in the streets of New York City. Not only do I decry wolf whistles and cat calling, I mention a once popular local man in the Adams Morgan district of Washington D.C. He made a mission out of complimenting women, and ensured they arrived home safely. I also bring up the dozens of copycats that spun their parodies to grab views on YouTube.

The Almighty Pat Robertson

I write up a short sketch describing the life of Pat Robertson. I also write about the suspect investment ventures involving the evangelist in other countries.

❧ The Block is Hot ☙

Lil' Wayne, a mainstream rap star, took his message to YouTube that his next album will be delayed for internal reasons. I'm not a huge fan of the artist, but I applaud his efforts to reach viewers on why he is who he is. And then he wants to think about why you behave the way you do, for whatever reasons. A public service announcement on how you should take time for making personal decisions.

❧ The Cassette Tape Culture ☙

If you grew up in the eighties, you may remember the cassette tape commercial by Memorex. I recount the days of how important cassette tapes were as an elementary school student and beyond. And how love for tapes shifted onto video tapes.

❧ The Chicano Movement ☙

Following podcast listenership, I tuned into the Brilliant Idiots. The two man team trade sarcasm over current events and have guests attend their shows from time to time. A particular personality was a radio jockey from California was of Chicano descent. Upon that knowledge, I start earmarking events that celebrate Chicano culture.

❧ The Crime Wizards of Oz ☙

A day in the life of a foodie. The moment I read about good news in the paper, I don't know who to email about it. A young girl's life was saved with a heart transplant. So I consider contacting the Tin Man from the Wizard of Oz since he's all about hearts. That discussion leads to interstate politics about governors. And his friends turned felons committing crimes.

᠆ᢀ The Food Babe ᢀ᠆

The ups and downs of a blogger cum activist that fights for the right for corporations to seriously reevaluate what ingredients they put into their products. Even if she fails to move industries to disclose once classified information, onlookers with a stronger reach may feel prompted to investigate various companies. Her shortfalls hinge on her spiritual beliefs, in this case pseudoscience.

᠆ᢀ The Holiday Scammers ᢀ᠆

Gift cards scams seem to sift out of notoriety depending on the holidays. Although they're seemingly legitimate, there tends to be bound by quirky strands of red tape on how and when to use them.

᠆ᢀ The Icarus Claus ᢀ᠆

At a second hand bookstore, I skim a old book of folk tales. I see the story of the boy that tried to travel to the Sun. As I read the story, I took a moment to wonder what if the father of Phaeton (Icarus) was St. Nick. Then I recounted the tale with a twist.

᠆ᢀ The Wonderful World of Doritos ᢀ᠆

I celebrate the world's most delicious corn tortilla chip. I touch upon the creator's death, submissions for a Frito-lay contest, and various chip flavors that are marketed worldwide.

᠆ᢀ These Colors Don't Run ᢀ᠆

Americans as a whole have a thousand reasons not to travel abroad. Typical ugly American attitudes. Although the world is worth seeing, America has plethora of sightseeing adventures to savor. And there's plenty of propaganda with negative images of the outside world. Despite our stereotypical stance, we adore all things international. We just express ourselves differently.

⤚⊙ Zone Out ⊙⤙

My tribute towards the Serling brainchild. Before Star Trek and the Star Wars franchise, there was the mesmerizing Twilight Zone series. I ramble on about the best episodes, the scores, and overall theme of most of their shows. Hats off to you, Rod Serling!

www.ingramcontent.com/pod-product-compliance
Lightning Source LLC
Chambersburg PA
CBHW070631030426
42337CB00020B/3983